Research Reports ESPRIT

Project 5660 · PECOS · Vol. 1

Edited in cooperation with
the Commission of the European Communities

W0245747

Editor

Richard J. D. Power
Artificial Intelligence Software spa
Via Rombon 11, I-20134 Milano, Italy

ESPRIT Exploratory Action 5660 "Perspectives on Cooperative Systems (PECOS)" belongs to the area Advanced Business and Home Systems — Peripherals of the ESPRIT Programme (European Specific Programme for Research and Development in Information Technology) supported by the European Communities.

The goal of the ESPRIT Exploratory Action 5660 (PECOS) was to investigate models for Computer Supported Cooperative Work (CSCW) with special reference to cooperation among organisations in large projects. The PECOS action included an evaluation of the state of the art as regards both technological capability and organisational theory and practice. New methodological proposals were made based on two practical contexts. The first was the management of a complex industrial project, the construction of a highspeed train for the Italian railway, which required cooperation among four private companies. The second was the design of an information system for water management in the Lombardy region, which required cooperation among several different branches of public administration. These contexts were studied, applying techniques of enterprise modelling, in order to identify requirements for CSCW systems. It was concluded that CSCW technology could facilitate a heterarchical style of management, particularly appropriate for complex industrial projects with an innovative product and time-based competition. The action suggests a methodology which emphasizes the importance of modelling the application context and integrating all tools into a common environment.

CR Subject Classification (1991): K.6, H.4, I.2

ISBN-13:978-3-540-56263-4   e-ISBN-13:978-3-642-84871-1
DOI: 10.1007/978-3-642-84871-1

Publication No. EUR 14818 EN of the
Commission of the European Communities,
Scientific and Technical Communication Unit,
Directorate-General Telecommunications, Information Industries and Innovation,
Luxembourg

LEGAL NOTICE
Neither the Commission of the European Communities nor any person acting on behalf of the Commission is responsible for the use which might be made of the following information.

© ECSC – EEC – EAEC, Brussels – Luxembourg, 1993

Typesetting: Camera ready by authors
45/3140 – 543210 – Printed on acid-free paper

R. J. D. Power (Ed.)

Cooperation Among Organizations

The Potential of
Computer Supported Cooperative Work

Springer-Verlag

Berlin Heidelberg New York
London Paris Tokyo
Hong Kong Barcelona
Budapest

Preface

This book reports research conducted in the ESPRIT project PECOS, which investigated the requirements for effective CSCW (Computer Supported Cooperative Work) with special reference to cooperation among organisations in large projects. It indicates commercial areas where CSCW technology can be applied, and examines such methodological issues as enterprise modelling, system architecture, and the incorporation of artificial intelligence techniques.

PECOS studied two practical contexts. The first was the management of a complex industrial project, the construction of a high-speed train for the Italian railway, which required cooperation among four private companies. The second was the design of an information system for water management in the Lombardy region, which required cooperation among several different branches of public administration. These contexts were analysed, applying techniques of enterprise modelling, in order to identify requirements for CSCW systems.

The composition of the book is as follows. Chapter 1 presents some highlights of the vast literature on cooperation, including results from psychology, sociology, management science, linguistics, and artificial intelligence. Chapter 2 reviews the much shorter history of CSCW, with reference to a catalogue of existing systems given in an appendix at the end of the book. The next four chapters contain our original findings. Chapter 3 describes the background to the two case studies. After a general introduction to enterprise modelling, Chapter 4 presents models of the case studies and discusses their implications in general terms. More detailed discussion follows in Chapters 5 and 6, which deal with intelligent computer support and the design of an appropriate system environment. Collecting together these various suggestions, there emerges a coherent methodology for CSCW which is described in Chapter 7.

PECOS (PErspectives on COoperative Systems) was an "exploratory action" - that is, a short project which investigates a promising new area of information technology without producing actual software. It began in October 1990 and lasted 12 months. The conception of the project owed much to Flavio Argentesi and Francesco Gardin, whom we would like to thank for their essential contribution. We would also like to express our gratitude to the project officer Fieny Pijls for her help and encouragement while the research was in progress.

The consortium of PECOS was made up of seven partners; names and addresses of authors are given at the end of the book.
- Artificial Intelligence Software (AIS), Milan, Italy (Coordinating partner)
- Babbage Institute (BIKIT), Ghent, Belgium
- EMMEPI - Fiatimpresit, Milan, Italy
- INTELSA, Madrid, Spain
- Lombardia Informatica, Milan, Italy
- MARI, Gateshead, Great Britain
- University of Madrid (UPM), Spain

December 1992   Richard Power

Contents

1 Cooperative work in organizations

Boudewijn D'Hauwers, Veerle Van Hyfte, Fernand Vandamme,
Richard Power

1. Introduction

If we want to achieve effective CSCW, we must understand how people work together
in organizations. The understanding required is both general and specific: at a general
level, we must be aware of any principles that apply widely across different contexts of
cooperative work; at a specific level, we need a set of concepts and procedures for
analysing particular contexts.

The study of cooperative work and organizations has of course a long history with
contributions from several disciplines, especially psychology, sociology, management
science, linguistics, and more recently artificial intelligence. Organizational behaviour
is a branch of social psychology which studies such questions as personal motivation,
job satisfaction, stress at work, group dynamics, conflict, leadership, communication,
and group decision making (Baron 1986). Although there is much overlap, social
psychology differs from sociology and management science in focussing more on the
perspective of the individual. The relevant branch of linguistics is pragmatics, which
deals with the relations between language and the context in which it is used (Levinson
1983). Finally, the discipline of distributed artificial intelligence has provided new
theoretical models by extending classical AI work on problem solving to contexts in
which problems are tackled by several agents (Bond & Gasser 1988).

In the present chapter we select from this vast field those topics which are
especially relevant for the design of CSCW systems. Section 2 reviews basic results
from linguistics and conversational analysis, especially speech act theory, which has
been applied by several authors (e.g. Winograd & Flores 1986) to the modelling of
communication patterns in cooperative work. Section 3 describes some empirical
results on organizational behaviour, with particular reference to group decision-making,
negotiation, and conferences. Finally, section 4 introduces the theoretical perspective of
distributed artificial intelligence.

2. Human communication

2.1 Speech act theory

Although historically speech acts were first studied by a philosopher (Austin 1962), they belong properly to pragmatics, the branch of linguistics which deals with the use of language as opposed to its structure (syntax) and meaning (semantics).

In his pioneering work, Austin pointed out that any normal utterance in a conversation performs simultaneously several conceptually distinct actions. Suppose that Mary says to John: "The printer is out of order". At a simple level her action consists merely in producing a sentence with a certain descriptive meaning: Austin called this a *locutionary* act. If she is speaking seriously (rather than practising her English for example), Mary's utterance will be interpreted as an attempt to achieve a purpose: in this case she performs not only a locutionary act but also an *illocutionary* act. Finally, if John believes she is sincere, Mary may achieve her purpose, in which case she performs also a *perlocutionary* act.

Austin arrived at this distinction by classifying literally hundreds of English verbs which can be used for reporting utterances. For instance, the verb SAY reports a locutionary act, since the sentence

"Mary said that the printer was out of order"

would remain true even if Mary was talking to herself in order perhaps to practise the idiom "out of order". Instead the verb INFORM reports an illocutionary act: the sentence

"Mary informed John that the printer was out of order"

implies that a social event took place in which Mary attempted, through her utterance, to add a particular fact to John's knowledge. However, it does not imply that she succeeded: perhaps John did not believe her. Finally, the verb CONVINCE reports a perlocutionary act, since for example the sentence

"Mary convinced John that the printer was out of order"

implies that Mary achieved her aim of updating John's knowledge.

Austin and later researchers paid particular attention to the analysis of illocutionary acts, which may be regarded as the basic moves of conversation. The concept of illocution is crucial because it expresses the difference between genuine conversation and mere recitation. To qualify as a contribution to a conversation, an utterance must be perceived as an attempt to achieve a social purpose. Austin hoped that by analysing the subtle differences of meaning among illocutionary verbs, much could be learned about the conceptual framework underlying human social behaviour.

Austin's program was taken further by Searle (1969), who tried to state necessary and sufficient conditions for the correct performance of various illocutionary acts. These conditions were grouped into three kinds: *content* conditions, which specify the appropriate descriptive content; *preparatory* conditions, which specify the appropriate circumstances; and *sincerity* conditions, which specify the appropriate attitudes by the speaker. For instance, the illocutionary act REQUEST has the following rules:

Content:	Future action A of hearer H.
Preparatory:	(a) H can do A; Speaker S believes H can do A.
	(b) H is not obviously going to do A anyway.
Sincerity:	S wants H to do A.

A final rule (which Searle calls the "Essential condition") states that a request counts as an attempt by S to get H to do A.

On the basis of such analyses Searle (1975) grouped illocutionary acts into five main categories:

Assertive:	Commit the speaker to a statement;
Directive:	Attempt to get the hearer to do something;
Commissive:	Commit the speaker to a future action;
Declaration:	Cause the propositional content to become true
	(e.g. "I now declare you man and wife");
Expressive:	Express a psychological state (e.g. apologize, praise).

An implication of Searle's approach is that utterances in a conversation can be understood only with reference to a social situation which is recognized by the participants. Although in special cases this situation is externalised - for instance through legal documents - in most cases it exists only in people's minds, like the board in a blindfold chess game. For example, there will usually be no document which proves that John owns a particular pencil: he owns it because the relevant people believe he does. (Of course this informal system is vulnerable to cheating: this is why for important matters we need the law.) Utterances do not directly manipulate physical objects like chairs and printers: they manipulate intangible mental or social entities such as beliefs, intentions, rights, and responsibilities.

Following up this insight, some researchers have used artificial intelligence planning formalisms in order to express the goal-subgoal structure of speech acts (Cohen & Perrault 1979, Power 1979). In these theories, utterances are seen as attempts to influence the beliefs and intentions of the hearer, but these mental attitudes may be embedded since each participant has beliefs/intentions about the beliefs/intentions of the other. In Cohen's elegant treatment, embedded attitudes are assigned to different "spaces": for instance, John's beliefs form a space which includes John's beliefs about Mary's beliefs, which in turn includes John's beliefs about Mary's beliefs about John's beliefs. Of special importance in social interaction are "mutual belief" spaces, which represent the common knowledge of two or more people (Lewis 1969).

As well as analysing single speech acts some suggestions have been made about how they are grouped into functional sequences. Schegloff & Sacks (1973) pointed out that utterances often come in pairs such as Question-Answer, Proposal-Response, Statement-Acknowledgement. This idea was developed by Power (1974) and Levin &

Moore (1978), who suggested the concept of a "Dialogue Game", a short social routine by which two or more agents can achieve complementary goals. More complex routines have been proposed by Winograd & Flores (1986), who use transition networks to represent the various paths that a conversational activity might follow.

2.2 Conversational analysis

During the late 1960s a group of sociologists (especially Garfinkel 1967) launched a new discipline called ethnomethodology, concerned with the precise yet implicit cultural rules which determine how behaviour in that culture is interpreted. As an example of this approach, a group led by Sacks began to transcribe and analyse naturally-occurring telephone conversations and to point out regularities in how these conversations were opened (Schegloff 1968) and closed (Schegloff & Sacks 1973), and in how the speaking turn was transferred from one participant to another (Sacks, Schegloff & Jefferson 1974). As more researchers took up this approach, the eccentric term "ethnomethodology" was gradually dropped in favour of "conversational analysis".

In his study on openings, Schegloff (1968) found that conversations between two people typically begin with a summons (e.g. John telephones Mary) and acknowledgement (Mary picks up the receiver and says "Hallo"): this exchange establishes that John wishes to talk with Mary for some unspecified purpose, and that Mary is willing to comply. Before getting down to business a brief personal aside is often introduced (John asks what Mary is doing; she replies that she was reading the newspaper): as well as confirming that Mary is available, this provides material for ending the conversation later on ("Well, I'll let you get back to your newspaper"). Then the first party establishes the main topic of the conversation (John asks whether Mary can come to a meeting) - it would be very odd if this was not done quickly.

In their study on closings, Schegloff & Sacks (1973) observed that the final act in a conversation is an exchange of idiomatic farewells such as "Good-bye", "See you"; these must be produced by both participants and must be temporally adjacent or even overlapping. If this exchange is interrupted, for instance because a participant suddenly introduces a new topic, then it must be recommenced later from the beginning, so that it is clear to all parties that at this precise moment they are all willing to terminate the interaction. Another interesting observation is that the final exchange cannot occur at any point in the conversation: it must be prepared, by what Schegloff & Sacks call a "pre-closing sequence". Such sequences serve to wind the conversation down gradually, providing a period in which the participants can ensure that no further topics need to be raised. In a conversation with several topics, a pre-closing sequence is often started by summarizing the outcome of the main topic. For instance, if John telephones Mary to ask whether a report is ready, but they go on to discuss some other matters, he might indicate a desire to close the conversation by saying "So, you'll be sending me the report next Monday". As mentioned above, pre-closing sequences can also be started by referring to whatever the participants were doing before the conversation: for instance, "I'd better get back to debugging my program". Another common method is to indicate the time or place when interaction will be resumed - "I expect I'll see you in the office tomorrow afternoon".

Openings and closings are interesting because they concern the regulation of the conversation itself, as distinguished from whatever activity the conversation promotes. If we look carefully at the patterns which occur in natural conversations, we find that they serve important purposes, such as ensuring that all relevant topics have been raised, or that everyone understands and accepts that the interaction should end now. Another important task of conversation management is the regulation of the speaking turn (Sacks, Schegloff & Jefferson 1974). In a synchronous conversation, at any moment one person should speak and the others should attend, confining their contributions to brief "back-channel responses" such as "Yes", "Uh-huh", "Okay". When the speaker has reached a point at which his/her present contribution could be considered complete, the speaking turn may in various ways be transferred to another participant. According to Sacks et al, the current speaker may select another participant, for instance by an addressed question. If no such technique is used, other participants can claim the floor simply by speaking up; if they forgo this opportunity, the current speaker may take another turn.

Conversational anaylsis is relevant to CSCW because to design new systems of communication we need to provide effective methods for regulating interactions. During a conference, it must be clear who is participating, when the conference began, what topic is currently under discussion, whether this is a main topic or a side topic, who currently holds the floor, when a topic is being closed, when the conference is moving towards its close, and when closure is imminent. Perhaps for asynchronous conferences the rules will be somewhat different - for instance, the concept of "holding the floor" may no longer apply, or may at least need to be modified; nevertheless, some kind of regulation will be needed, and the computer support must be designed so that this regulation is accomplished easily and without conscious effort.

3. Behaviour in organizations

3.1 Group decision-making

Group dynamics has been a topic of major interest in social psychology and management science since the 1920s (Baron 1986). When people participate in a group, they often orient towards a group perspective which may differ from their private views, or the attitudes they adopt in other groups. This tendency has dangers as well as advantages: it can lead to irresponsibile behaviour (e.g. football hooliganism), or to unrealistic decision-making.

Many studies have shown that decisions made by groups are more extreme or more risky than decisions made by individuals (Stoner 1961). This and other unrealistic tendencies have been called "groupthink" (Janis 1982). Some typical symptoms of groupthink are the following:

(i) *Illusion of invulnerability:* over-optimism leads to taking extreme risks and overlooking obvious danger signs.

(ii) *Collective rationalization:* Warnings that run contrary to group thinking are discredited or ignored.

(iii) *Unquestioned morality:* The group position is assumed to be ethical because nobody present questions it.

(iv) *Excessive negative stereotyping:* Because of its excessive optimism and confidence, the group assumes that opposing views do not warrant serious consideration.

(v) *Self-censorship of dissenting ideas:* Members of the group keep dissenting ideas to themselves so as not to damage group cohesiveness.

(vi) *Illusion of unanimity:* Because dissent tends to remain unexpressed, members of the group overestimate the degree of unanimity.

When people are brought together in a group, they gradually accumulate a distinctive culture, including norms of behaviour which are established by precedents and critical events, or imported by members from other contexts (Feldman 1984). Roles within the group become differentiated. Early studies (e.g. Benne & Sheats 1948) found that people tended to contribute either as task specialists or as social specialists: the former role includes actions directly relevant to getting the job done, such as providing information or suggesting a plan; the latter role is oriented towards promoting group cohesion and personal satisfaction, for instance by smoothing over conflicts or by giving praise or encouragement.

In management science, the classical view of decision making has been that people reach decisions by formulating options and calculating their consequences. If complete information is available, this process is called "optimizing"; if not, it is called "satisficing" (a concept introduced by AI pioneer Herbert Simon, who received the Nobel prize in Economics for his work on decision-taking under uncertainty). According to more recent approaches, decision-taking is governed by the search for appropriate normative rules. Instead of calculating consequences, people often ask: "What should a person like me do in a situation like this?" In other words, they seek a social rule which applies to the present situation.

Managers actually spend little time taking decisions: their main activities are monitoring and interpretation. Empirical studies have shown that managers devote much time to praising, blaming, socializing, and joking. They also indulge in long political disputes over how previous decisions and their consequences should be interpreted. Senior managers devote most of their time to face-to-face communication. Reder & Schwab (1990) compared senior managers with other staff (developers, marketing). Other staff spent at least 50% of time doing solitary work. Managers devoted only 15% to solitary work and 60% to face-to-face interaction with colleagues.

On average, managers were interrupted once every four minutes. If we want to design effective computer support for group decision making, it is important that these typical patterns of work are observed and understood.

3.2 Negotiation

Negotiation is a group interaction which aims to resolve a decision problem on which the participants have different perspectives and competing preferences and interests. During the negotiation, consensus is built through such actions as compromises, trade-offs, bargaining, and mutual concessions. From the viewpoint of individual participants, the problems presented by negotiation are partly cognitive and partly political. At a cognitive level, a special effort may be needed in order to understand the positions of other parties, who may use unfamiliar concepts, or may see the matter from another perspective so that different factors become relevant. At a political level, each participant tries to understand the motives, strengths, and weaknesses of the others, so as to manoeuvre towards a consensus position that satisifies their own interests.

In most negotiations a crucial role is played by the mediator, an impartial agent whose job is to clarify the various positions and to seek ways of achieving consensus. Expert mediators apply a number of techniques which have been described by Pruitt (1981).

(i) *Cost cutting:* a participant may agree to relax a constraint if some way can be found of reducing the associated cost.

(ii) *Cost sharing:* one way of cutting the cost associated with a constraint is to share it among all the parties. For example, a company polluting a river might agree to purify the waste if the cost of doing so was shared by the organizations that benefitted from cleaner water.

(iii) *Log rolling:* this refers to an exchange of concessions, so that the conditions previously laid down by each agent are satisfied in part. The mediator should establish, for each agent, an order of priority for constraints, so that solutions can be proposed which violate only constraints of lower priority.

(iv) *Bridging:* This is a variant of log rolling in which the mediator develops a new option which satisfies the main constraints of all parties.

(v) *Unlinking:* When progress has been blocked because each party insists on a complex set of linked conditions, the mediator may try to separate these links, so that the matter is resolved into a number of smaller issues that can be tackled one at a time.

(vi) *Arbitration:* If consensus cannot be reached, the parties may as a last resort agree to accept the verdict of an external arbitrator.

Although an attempt has been made to create an expert system that mediates using these techniques (Sathi et al 1986), in most contexts mediation requires a common-sense understanding of the domain which cannot yet be built into a computer program. A more realistic aim is to provide tools to support a human mediator. Several existing tools might be adapted to this purpose. First of all, a hypertext system like gIBIS (Conklin et al 1988) would be useful for representing the positions of the participants in a standard explicit format. Second, once a position has been defined, the mediator and the other participants should be able to attach queries and comments (see for example the ForComment system, Opper 1988). Third, the mediator will need to merge sections of each position in order to construct compromise proposals. Finally, support should be provided for recording the history of the negotiation, so that the current situation is clear to all parties, and previous assertions or commitments can be reconstructed in case of doubt.

3.3 Meetings and conferences

Numerous studies have testified that the most important activity in cooperative work is communication. Software developers for example may spend as much as 80% of their time interacting with colleagues and only 20% working on the computer. Kedsiersky (1982) observed a team working on a small development project. On average, about 80% of time was spend in formal/informal meetings or on the phone (27% questioning, 25% informing, 13% complaining, 14% planning/discussing). Communication was identified both as the main activity and the main cause of problems.

From research in social psychology, and reports based on practical experience, a good deal of advice has been accumulated on how to communicate effectively and on how to run meetings. Meetings may be classified by purpose, frequency, attendance, and by the protocol observed. When organizing a meeting, a primary task is to define its purpose clearly; this sounds obvious, but often it is not done. Some common purposes are the following: exchange information, coordinate activities, make decisions, find out opinions, propose solutions, educate or train, formulate policy, and encourage creative thinking.

In addition to the purpose, some other elements of a meeting are the agenda, the leader (chairperson, facilitator), and the secretary (recorder). All these elements should be determined at the outset. The agenda should contain a brief statement of purpose, a list of topics to be discussed, and a schedule of the time allotted to each topic. When the meeting is over, it should be followed up: minutes should be circulated, and any new actions or responsibilities decided at the meeting should be clearly defined. In some cases, a report should be prepared for other interested groups.

Leader behaviour has been intensively studied (for a review see Baron 1986, chapter 9). Broadly speaking, two styles can be distinguished: participative and autocratic. Which style is more effective depends on the task, and on whether efficiency is considered more important than job satisfaction. Participative leaders are usually preferred by subordinates, and so enhance organizational commitment; the disadvantages of this style are that decisions tend to be made more slowly, and the competence of the leader may be called into question. Autocratic leaders tend to reach quick decisions, and hence to enhance productivity, especially for high-pressure tasks, but on the negative side they reduce job satisfaction and fail to exploit fully the skills of their subordinates.

Whatever style is adopted, the leader of a meeting should be objective, and able to control the discussion by eliciting comments and summarizing at appropriate moments. The leader need not be a major expert, but should at least be familiar with the topic; in addition, he/she should have an interest in the outcome of the meeting, and know when to stop. It has been found that successful leaders are sensitive to colleagues and changing conditions, and have a strong concern both for people and quality; they are flexible and not afraid of being influenced by others, being participative or autocratic in varying degrees as the situation demands.

The detailed running of the discussion at a meeting varies according to the type of activity. For problem solving, the discussion could be organized as follows:

State the problem clearly
Identify the causes of the problem
Identify the obstacles
Generate alternative solutions
Evaluate the alternative solutions
Develop a plan of action.

For an activity of decision analysis the following steps would be appropriate:

Fix objectives
Establish priorities among objectives
Develop alternative solutions and evaluate them
Make a tentative choice
Think of things that might go wrong
Make contingency plans to deal with possible mishaps.

Another common activity is the analysis of potential problems, which can be approached as follows:

Develop a plan of action
List potential problems
Assess the resulting risks
Identify the causes of the problems
Assess their probabilities
Find ways of preventing the events that cause problems
Define a plan for dealing with the main problem
Establish control procedures.

In conclusion, it should be noted that the person who runs a meeting need not be the same as the person who has decisional power. In many cases it may be useful to dissociate these roles: the facilitator runs the meeting, using expertise in methodology; decisions about the problem domain are made by the whole group, or by a manager, or by the person with most technical competence. For complex technical discussions among representatives from several organizations, there are obvious reasons why the meeting should be chaired by an external facilitator rather than by a manager or technical expert, who may be seen as favouring the interests of his/her own organization rather than the interests of the whole project.

4. Distributed artificial intelligence

Most artificial intelligence research investigates how a single agent can exhibit intelligent behaviour, such as solving problems using heuristic or knowledge-based methods, planning, perception, learning, and natural language understanding and production. Several recent developments have together provoked interest in concurrency and distribution in AI: the development of powerful concurrent (cooperative) computers, the proliferation of multinode computer networks, and the recognition that much human problem solving and activity involves groups of people.

There is now some understanding of how a single agent can solve problems, but this work must be extended to cover knowledge representation and planning with several agents. The presence of multiple agents is seen as an unavoidable condition of the real world. People must cooperate taking into account the potential actions of others. The technology of DAI should help groups or organizations to communicate information faster, more cheaply, and more effectively. To take advantage of these new strategies and operational possibilities, we need major extensions or reformulations of current theories of organizations, markets, and management. This is also something which is discussed in DAI applications, which offer new systems that can support people in all sorts of cooperative work.

Bond & Gasser (1990) divide the field of DAI into the following three areas:

(i) *Distributed Problem Solving (DPS):* Research in DPS considers how the work of solving a particular problem can be divided among a number of modules, or "nodes", that cooperate at the level of dividing and sharing knowledge about the problem and about the developing solution.

(ii) *Multi-agent systems (MA):* Research here is concerned with coordinating intelligent behaviour among a collection of autonomous intelligent "agents", and in how they can coordinate their knowledge, goals, skills and plans jointly to take action or to solve problems. The agents in a multi-agent system may be working toward a single global goal, or toward separate individual goals that interact. Agents in a multi-agent system must share knowledge about problems and solutions. But they must also reason about the process of coordination among the agents. In multi-agent systems, the task of coordination can be quite difficult, for there may be situations (in so called open systems) where there is no possibility for global control, globally consistent knowledge, globally shared goals or global success criteria, or even a global representation of a system.

(iii) *Parallel AI (PAI):* Research in this area is concerned with developing parallel computer architectures, languages, and algorithms for AI. These are primarily directed toward solving the performance problems of AI systems, and not toward conceptual advances in understanding the nature of reasoning and intelligent behaviour among multiple agents.

Within the literature on DAI the following approaches can be distinguished:

(i) *Natural system approach:* This studies the strategies and representations that people use to coordinate their activities, in much the same way that cognitive scientists investigate individual cognition in people. It includes computer modelling and simulation of the coordination activities of people.

(ii) *Engineering science perspective:* In this case one investigates how to build functioning, automated, coordinated problem solvers for specific applications. Bond & Gasser suggest that the problems of coordination and cooperation would be simplified by using standard communication protocols and by relying upon global viewpoints.

(iii) *Person-machine coordination approach:* This perspective would be useful in analyzing and developing collections of people and machines working together in coordinated ways. Especially in this approach, research in DAI is already seeding research and practice in the area of computer supported cooperative work.

Research in the field of DAI can contribute to the development of computer support for cooperative work. Examples of relevant work in DAI are the following:

(i) Analysis of the interaction processes that occur in cooperative work.

(ii) Strategies of cooperation dealing with different aspects such as the problem of dividing the tasks, and how to tackle incompleteness and uncertainty in information. These strategies have been studies in particular for the context of problem solving and decision making. Specific protocols are presented, with special attention to the (simple or multi-stage) negotiation protocol that is useful for resolving resource allocation conflicts.

(iii) Architectures and languages in DAI indicate a trend towards flexible implementation frameworks, such as heterogeneous, multigrain problem-solving frameworks, and also towards language and system support for flexible organization and cooperation structures. The field of DAI is still searching for a balance between social and technological issues. Computer support for groups implies more than merely developing new applications. Many other problems arise, such as how to manage distributed databases with which multiple user groups on different organizational levels and locations must interact. It is not sufficient to apply theories from the behavioural sciences to computer contexts, for two reasons. First, there are some qualitatively new phenomena, such as the cooperative intelligent behaviour that results when cognition is distributed among diverse group members and when intelligence (or information) is shared by people and machines. Second, there are also phenomena which, although present in other contexts, assume a new level of importance.

Early computer programs bore little resemblance to human organizations, but as the problems attacked grew in size, resource limitations began to invalidate previously successful programmed solutions. Some work in artificial intelligence can be viewed as an attempt to circumvent such resource limitations. Also in the area of cooperative work facilitated with the computer, more and more emphasis is being given to theories of groups or organizations. Hence one finds "intelligent" programs (e.g. Hearsay II) which also display characteristics of human organizations (Lesser & Erman 1980). These trends have resulted in modules that contain problem-solving characteristics similar to humans. The field of cooperative distributed problem solving will be described more fully in chapter 5.

2 Computer Supported Cooperative Work

Richard Power, Lorella Carminati

1. Overview

The concept of computer supported cooperative work (CSCW) was pioneered by Engelbart, who demonstrated as early as 1968 a prototype called NLS/Augment. Developed at the Stanford Research Institute during the period 1963-76, this system allowed office workers to communicate either by exchanging documents or by interacting in real time through a shared window. Part of the philosophy behind NLS/Augment was that interaction with computers should be made as simple and natural as possible: to this end Engelbart introduced such features as windows, mixed text and graphics, pop-up menus, and the mouse.

Until 1980, interest in CSCW was limited to a few visionaries like Engelbart, but thereafter the field expanded rapidly. The first workshop was held at MIT in 1984, and major conferences followed in 1986, 1988, and 1990 (Greif 1988, Bikson 1990). These conferences attracted researchers from a wide range of disciplines including computer science, artificial intelligence, psychology, sociology, and management science. Towards the end of the 1980s a centre for Coordination Science was established at MIT, and some early CSCW products began to reach the market. Many of these products are cited in the December 1988 issue of "Byte", which features a special report on Groupware. A journal dedicated to CSCW (Journal of Organizational Computing) was founded in 1991.

Since CSCW is a new field, it does not yet have clear boundaries or a clear internal organization. At the most recent large conference (CSCW-90, Los Angeles) the presentations were grouped as follows (Bikson, 1990):

Shared video spaces
Experimental studies in CSCW
Supporting structured communication
CSCW within and across organizations
CSCW applications
Cooperative support and customization

      User interfaces in the CSCW context
      CSCW in the field
      Systems infrastructure for CSCW
      Issues and perspectives on CSCW.

Although fragmentary this does at least indicate the scope of the field. A more fundamental partition can be derived from the acronym itself, which divides conveniently into CS (Computer Support) and CW (Cooperative Work). In Chapter 1 we reviewed the contributions of several disciplines, especially social psychology and management science, to the understanding of cooperative work - a topic with a long history. The present chapter instead focusses on the experimental computer systems which have appeared over the last few years.

We begin in section 2 by listing, with brief explanations, the features that have so far been employed in CSCW systems. Section 3 describes in more detail some representative systems, selected from a longer list which we present in catalogue form in the appendix. Section 4 reports some empirical studies on the behaviour and opinions of users. Finally, in section 5, some conclusions are drawn about the current state of the art, with particular reference to our aim of providing effective computer support for complex projects in which the activities of several organizations must be coordinated.

2. Features of existing CSCW systems

The catalogue of CSCW applications in the appendix contains systems of very diverse kinds. Some offer a complete range of services while others are special-purpose tools. Some are large commercial products while others are small research prototypes. Some remain within conventional information technology while others employ expert systems or other methods from artificial intelligence. Thus to show what has been accomplished it is not sufficient simply to describe one or two representative applications. Our aim in the present section is to cover the field by collecting together the ideas so far incorporated into CSCW systems.

a) Synchronous communication

This means communication in real time, as occurs in a conversation face-to-face or over the telephone. Many office automation systems allow the immediate reception of messages typed in at the keyboard, perhaps through a shared window. Some experimental systems like MERMAID (Watabe et al 1990) allow people working in different cities to converse through an audio-visual link. Each participant is filmed and may appear in windows on other workstations. The audio link allows more than two participants to take part in the conversation, and provides a sound quality far superior to telephone. Of course a high-quality audio-visual link is at present too expensive for most applications.

b) Asynchronous communication

In this case there is a time lag between production and reception, as occurs with a telefax message or with electronic mail. Most systems requiring communication at a distance use electronic mail in preference to an audio-visual link for reasons of cost. Obviously asynchronous communication is slower, but it has some compensating advantages: sender and receiver can communicate even if they work at different times; if the material is complex there is no pressure to respond too quickly; in group discussions people who are usually too slow or too timid to capture the floor have a chance to contribute.

c) Same location

When people work in the same office, they can be coordinated by a local area network. Most office automation systems are of this type. In some cases it is further assumed that the participants are in the same room - see especially the computerized meeting room project COLAB (Stefik et al 1987).

d) Distant locations

To support cooperative work among groups at remote locations a wide area network is needed, in addition to local area networks at each site.

e) Shared windows

A shared window can be viewed and modified by two or more users at separate terminals, according to the principle of WYSIWIS (What you see is what I see). Typically, each user can display the shared window along with further private windows which will vary from one terminal to another. The person holding the floor can write into the window, the results being immediately visible to the other participants.

f) Document management

CSCW systems present some special problems of document management. Very large libraries of documents must be organized for efficient access and maintenance. Documents may have multiple authors and complex rules of access.

g) Versioning

When a document has several authors it will typically exist in multiple versions, as successive drafts are bounced back and forth for revision and for the insertion of new material. Some office automation systems (e.g. NLS/Augment) have special facilities for keeping track of multiple versions and optimizing storage of overlapping documents.

h) Multiple comments on document

For cooperative writing, coauthors often need to make comments on the original draft, or perhaps even comments on each other's comments. The ForComment system allows multiple reviewers to annotate a document, viewing and amplifying each other's remarks without corrupting the original version.

i) Data security
If a CSCW system is employed in order to coordinate a large project, loss of data represents a catastrophe equivalent to a fire in an office based on paper. Exceptional measures are needed to ensure that data are not corrupted either by accident or malice. These include the efficient production of backups, the authorisation of users, access management, and in some cases cryptographic support.

j) Multimedia documents
Asynchronous communication in particular is enhanced if users can create and send multimedia documents. The Diamond system (Thomas et al 1985) allows authors to compose documents with text, diagrams, photographs, and recorded speech. By clicking on an icon the receiver can hear the spoken message.

k) Multiple tasks
Office workers typically have a stack of unfinished tasks, since activities are often interrupted by pressure from colleagues. Office automation systems (e.g. WordPerfect Office) usually allow users to keep several tasks open at once and to switch easily from one to another.

l) Email link
Most office automation systems facilitate the sending of documents by electronic mail.

m) Routing to telex or fax
Office Works, among other systems, allows users to route messages to electronic mail, telex, or fax. The sender can simply instruct the system to send message X to person Y by route Z, and the system takes care of the rest, trying later if the connection is currently occupied.

n) Semi-structured messages
Some researchers claim that messages sent internally or by electronic mail can be processed more effectively if they are "semi-structured" - that is, if as well as free text they contain some fields with information in a fixed format which the system can interpret. Information Lens (Malone et al 1987) is an example of a system with semi-structured messages and services that exploit this structure.

o) Speech act indexing
Systems like "The Coordinator" (Winograd 1988) and Strudel (Shepherd et al 1990) employ semi-structured messages with fields specifying the speech act category of a message and hence its role in the conversation.

p) Conversation management

Speech act indexing makes possible a further service in which related sequences of messages are grouped into "conversations"; by applying knowledge about conversational structure the system can draw inferences about the options available to the user and the commitments so far adopted.

q) Support for organizing ideas

In group discussions it is useful to have tools for visualising and organizing ideas. Cognoter (Stefik et al 1987), a tool for the COLAB computerized meeting room, supports brainstorming sessions in which participants add ideas to a shared window. In subsequent phases these ideas can be linked by drawing arrows or can be located on different hierarchical levels.

r) Representation of discussion

Systems like gIBIS (Conklin et al 1988) and SIBYL (Lee 1990) facilitate the representation of discussions, by providing standard categories for single contributions and for relations between them. For instance, the IBIS method distinguishes "issues" (which state questions or problems), "positions" (which state possible resolutions of issues), and "arguments" (which justify or criticize positions).

s) Negotiation support

Given a system for representing discussions, it is possible to add further tools for supporting negotiation. These tools would facilitate the task of the mediator, who must try to construct a coherent agreed position from the contradictory positions advanced by the participants. If these positions can be expressed in a formal notation, the system itself may be able to play the role of mediator (see the Callisto system, Rathi et al 1986).

t) Office procedure modelling

SCOOP (Ellis et al 1980) provides a formalism for modelling the procedures of an office. Once the tasks are defined, the system can monitor the current activities, perform automatic tasks when appropriate, and remind people of what they should be doing.

u) Computerised assistants

The experimental system COKES (Kaye et al) provides each user with a computerized assistant to which certain tasks can be delegated. Thus if Mary wants to fix a meeting with John by the end of the week, she can delegate this job to her assistant, which will get in contact with John's assistant, compare their forthcoming commitments, determine a convenient time, and add the new appointment to both agendas.

v) Project management support

Already in NLS/Augment, support was provided for maintaining a common work plan in project management. More ambitiously, Callisto (Rathi et al 1986) includes an expert system which can apply expertise on project management in order to support planning and negotiation.

w) Group consensus analysis

Régnier's Abacus is a tool for displaying the attitudes of a group of people towards a set of issues. First a list of perhaps 30 statements is compiled. Beside each statement there is a grid of seven responses, coded by colour in a scheme resembling traffic lights (Green affirmative, Red negative, Orange neutral, White means "Can't answer", Black means "Won't answer"). Each member in the group of perhaps 20 people provides a response to each statement. The whole set of attitudes is displayed through a 20x30 grid in which single responses are represented by coloured rectangular pixels. Using this method of display, global trends and local patterns leap immediately to the eye.

x) Group planning support

Several systems exploit Artificial Intelligence work on planning in order to represent and reason about group plans. Omega (Barber 1981) checks whether goals entered by the user are compatible with the goals of others in the group. Polymer (Croft et al 1988) uses an internal representation of common office procedures in order to suggest plans and to coordinate group behaviour.

y) Group scheduling

Among various tools in this category we will mention as an example the Visual Scheduler (Beard et al 1990), which represents individual schedules by a diagram in which busy periods are black and free periods are white. By superimposing the individual schedules of all the people in a group, the coordinator can distinguish periods when most people are free (light grey) from periods when most people are busy (dark grey).

3. Representative CSCW systems

3.1 Callisto

The CALLISTO project (Sathi et al 1986) was initiated by the Digital Equipment Corporation in 1981 with the aim of supporting the management of large engineering projects. At first the intention was to incorporate knowledge about project management into an expert system, to be used by a single user. In a subsequent phase of the project, a simplified version of the expert system (Mini-Callisto) was developed into a distributed system that would support negotiations about the scheduling of activities and resources.

In their observations on the first prototype, the authors explain why a distributed system was found to be valuable. "In relation to planning, it was noted that plans evolve through negotiations and are not prespecified. For example, negotiations are often used to allocate slack time. The project support system should model and support negotiations on slack time and associated revisions in the plan rather than assume fixed durations and generate slack time as in PERT/CPM models" (Greif 1988, p. 287).

Thus the distributed system contains knowledge about negotiation as well as knowledge about project management. For instance, it knows about such negotiating techniques as cost cutting, log rolling, bridging, unlinking, mediation, arbitration (Greif 1988, pp. 291-292). On simple issues, the relevant Mini-Callistos can negotiate a solution automatically: this is possible because activities and resources are represented formally. Obviously the system cannot support negotiation outside this formal domain, since this would require common sense reasoning and natural language understanding.

Although the CALLISTO project was perhaps over-ambitious, it produced an important general idea: namely, that the standard PERT/CPM methods for project management need to be supplemented by facilities for supporting discussion. PERT/CPM techniques work well provided that the activities, resources, and constraints are correctly specified; the trouble is that for complex projects this can only be done with considerable discussion and negotiation among the participants.

3.2 Cognoter

Cognoter is a tool developed by Stefik et al (1987) for COLAB, an experimental computerized meeting room at Xerox PARC. The meeting room is designed for use by up to six people. Each user has a workstation with video and keyboard, linked to the other workstations through a local area network. For presentations there is also a large touch-sensitive screen and a stand-up keyboard. Normally the contents of the large screen will appear on each individual workstation in a public window, but users can also run applications in private windows which will vary from one workstation to another.

Starting from this basic configuration, specific tools have been developed to support the various activities that take place during a meeting. Cognoter is a tool which facilitates the collective preparation of an article or presentation. It is assumed that this activity will have three phases. First of all, the group has a brainstorming session in which ideas are generated in any order without criticism. Next, the ideas are organized. Finally, they are evaluated.

Ideas generated during brainstorming are written into a shared window where they are represented by short titles. Fuller descriptions can be associated with each title: normally these are not displayed, but by clicking on the title they can be called up if necessary. New ideas may be added simlutaneously by several participants; existing ideas may be edited or moved around the window, but not deleted.

When enough ideas have been generated, the organization phase starts. This consists partly in arranging the ideas in a linear order, and partly in clustering so that some ideas are subordinated to others. Linear order is indicated graphically by directed arcs from one idea to the next. Clusters of ideas may be shifted to separate boards so that a distinction is drawn between main points and details.

In the evaluation phase the presentation plan is put into its final form. Irrelevant or mistaken ideas are deleted, new ideas are introduced if gaps are found in the argument, and ideas which were previously unclear, or badly expressed, are reworked until they are formulated to everyone's satisfaction.

Although the computerized meeting room is an extreme example of synchronous communication between people located in the same place, the methods used in Cognoter could be applied also in a distributed asynchronous system. Obviously an asynchronous meeting would last longer - probably days rather than hours - but the three phases of brainstorming, organization, and evaluation remain relevant, and the tools for writing ideas on to a public board, arranging them in linear order, and grouping them into clusters, could work in essentially the same way.

3.3 Coordinator

The Coordinator is a system for coordinating office work by conversations held over a computer network. It was built by Action Technologies and runs on a local area network of IBM-compatible personal computers. The philosophy behind the system was formulated by Winograd and Flores (1986) in their book "Understanding Computers and Cognition". This book argues that the design of computer software should be adapted better to human nature. With rare exceptions existing software imposes the paradigm of solitary problem-solving, whereas in reality most work is carried out in cooperation with other people through conversation.

The Coordinator exploits some current work in linguistics about the structure of conversation. Each message is associated with a speech act category - it might for instance be a request, or a proposal, or a promise - and the system has a repertory of networks which indicate the paths that a conversation may follow. Thus if X sends Y a question, Y is expected to provide an answer. On noting that the question has been asked, the system is able to infer that an answer should be provided, and to add this to Y's list of current commitments. Such facilities are of course based on a very superficial understanding of the conversation. The system cannot understand the content of the question, which is expressed in free text, but knows only that it belongs to the category "question" and should therefore receive in reply a message belonging to the category "answer".

Through the Coordinator, interaction by electronic mail is enhanced in two ways: first, messages belonging to the same exchange are clustered together, so that subsequently they are easier to find and to interpret; secondly, the system can provide some simple services based on its superficial representation of the structure of the conversation. Whether people need or want this kind of support remains unclear: Bullen et al (1990) found that many users of the Coordinator selected the "request" category for every message simply because it was the first item on the menu.

3.4 gIBIS

When people take technical decisions on their own, or in face-to-face conversation with colleagues, the rationale underlying the decision is usually recorded only partially, if at all, and may be completely forgotten later. To prevent this loss of valuable information, some researchers have suggested special formats by which the rationale can be coded. As a useful side effect these formats also oblige users to think out the issue more carefully. For example, instead of being satisfied with the first solution that comes to mind, they are obliged to state all the main alternatives and to give reasons for preferring one to the others.

A simple but effective method for representing the rationale underlying decisions is the IBIS format. IBIS stands for "Issue Based Information System". The basic idea is to distinguish three types of contribution to a discussion: ISSUES (which state questions or problems), POSITIONS (which state possible resolutions of issues), and ARGUMENTS (which justify or criticize positions). Conklin et al (1988) have developed a groupware system called gIBIS (Graphical IBIS) which enables users to create, through a graphical interface, a hypertext with nodes and links corresponding to IBIS concepts. Tools of this kind may prove useful in organizing complex asynchronous discussions.

The IBIS method may seem trivially simple, but according to Burgess & Conklin (1990) complex models of rationale have the disadvantage of being harder to learn and use. Toulmin's book "The Uses of Argument" (1969) suggested a more articulated formalism for representing discussions. At MIT, Lee (1990) has developed an even more powerful DRL (decision representation language) for the SIBYL system, with semantic links like "supports", "achieves", "queries", "subgoal of", "best alternative for", "component procedure of", and many others. However, with so many categories to choose from, users would need a great deal of training in order to represent discussions correctly.

3.5 Information Lens

Information Lens (Malone et al 1987) is an intelligent system for sharing information in organizations. The interface enables authors to create "semi-structured messages", which are frame-like objects with slots for time, place, speaker, topic, as well as fields containing normal free text. Slots may vary according to the type of message. By exploiting information in fixed format, the system enables the receiver to sort messages into folders by such criteria as sender, date, location, topic. Authors can send messages to a special mail box labelled "Anyone", from where it will automatically be redistributed to any user who declares an interest in the topic.

Information Lens resembles the Coordinator in that it tries to enhance electronic mail by adding to each message some compulsory fields in fixed format. The fixed format information enables the system to organize messages in the database, to retrieve them later, and to provide other special services. Although simple, this is a powerful idea which should prove especially effective in complex contexts. There is some evidence (Bullen et al 1990) that users dislike the chore of filling in the fixed format fields: such attitudes might change if the cooperative project involved several organizations and hundreds of people.

3.6 Mermaid

Developed by Watabe et al (1990) at NEC, Japan, the MERMAID system is an impressive experiment in synchronous remote communication through several media. The system runs on UNIX workstations which are linked at each site by a local area network, and at remote sites by a wide area network. In addition to the usual video, keyboard, and mouse, each workstation is equipped with some special hardware items: a videocamera attached above the screen so that it films the user's face; a microphone and speaker to provide a high quality audio link; an image scanner; and an electronic writing pad.

With this equipment, users in different cities can hold conversations in the same auditory space, with a sound quality far superior to the telephone. Documents or photographs or films can be presented on the screen through a system based on X-windows. Thus in a conversation between people located in different cities, each participant can display a film of the other person's face in a window, so that teleconferencing is achieved. If the discussion concerns a physical object, an industrial component perhaps, this object can be shown to all participants by holding it in front of the videocamera; or if it is a photograph or a page from a book, it can be shown with better resolution by using the image scanner.

At present, systems like MERMAID are too expensive for most application areas because they require a high-speed data network to transmit high-quality sound and video.

3.7 Office Works

Office Works is a recent example of an office automation system, a step in the direction of the office without paper. It runs on IBM-compatible personal computers in a local area network. The system should be linked to devices like the telephone and fax machine so that calls are dialled automatically and documents can be sent by fax without producing a version on paper.

To illustrate the operation of the system, we can assume that a telephone message arrives for someone who is out of the office. Instead of writing down a note on a slip of paper, the secretary will create a corresponding electronic message (on the screen this will look like the familiar paper note), assign it an urgency code, and put it in the receiver's mail box. If the message has top priority, it will be displayed with a beeping tone as soon as the receiver returns to his/her office and switches on the computer.

To take another example, suppose that the user wants to send a document to a group of people, of whom some work in the office, some work elsewhere but can be reached by electronic mail, and some can be reached only by fax. If the database has the necessary information (i.e. the workstation identifiers for people in the office, and the email or fax numbers of people outside), the user can simply issue a general instruction and the system will take care of the details.

4. Empirical studies of user behaviour

Some behavioural studies have investigated how people use existing groupware. Most of these studies focus on electronic mail, which is the only feature of CSCW technology that has so far been widely used. We list below some of the main findings.

(a) Messages sent by electronic mail tend not to reflect features of the social context, such as differences in status between author and recipient. Sproull & Kiesler (1986) found that email messages omitted information about the sender's location, department, status, age, and sex. People preferred to use electronic mail to send messages to superiors, not to subordinates.

(b) Compared with normal conversation, email behaviour is self-absorbed, uninhibited, and non-conformist. Sproull & Kiesler (1986) also found that messages focussed more on the sender's interests than the receiver's; wierd or obscene expressions were common; 40% of all messages were totally unrelated to work.

(c) Among users, the most popular groupware facility by far is that of sending messages in free format. Bullen & Bennett (1990) studied user reactions to the most common existing groupware products. Even when many other functions were supported, most users quickly learned how to send and receive messages but ignored everything else. For example, the "Coordinator" system allows message senders to specify a speech act category (e.g. Request, Inform). Often users selected "Request" merely because it was the first item on the menu, regardless of the actual content of the message.

(d) Many users like the facility through which messages could be linked into related groups. Some systems allow users to classify messages by content, so that receivers find their mail folders already organized in sections. Without this facility, people complain about the difficulty of tracking down related messages (Bullen & Bennett 1990).

(e) Users prefer tools that correspond to familiar activities. Electronic mail is accepted easily because it is like a letter, but faster. Learning new methods takes effort; people will invest this effort only if they anticipate large benefits (Bullen & Bennett 1990).

5. Conclusions

Research and development on CSCW is confined almost entirely to the last decade. Although most CSCW applications have so far been experimental systems developed in research laboratories, there are already several dozen serious products on the market, most of them office automation systems which run on local area networks. During the 1990s, as telecommunications improve and become cheaper, there will almost certainly be a rapid expansion of teleworking and of CSCW systems for coordinating work at remote sites.

Borrowing the terminology of the Cognoter system, we might characterize the current state of the CSCW field as one of brainstorming. Many ingenious ideas have been generated in research laboratories and tried out in experimental systems, but as yet there are few established issues and even fewer definite conclusions. Perhaps we have now reached a point at which more emphasis should be given to analysis and evaluation.

In this project we are specifically interested in CSCW systems that support collaboration among organizations in complex projects. Referring to the list in section 2, we can already identify some features that such a system would require. At each site, people will have access to terminals which are connected by a local area network. These local networks will be linked by a wide area network for transmitting documents and other data. For the next few years, the cost of transmitting voice and video film will probably be too high for most applications; we may therefore assume that remote communication will be asynchronous. Users will be able to create documents, usually in a partially structured format, which will either be sent as messages or be linked to a communal plan, report, or discussion. The system for managing documents must include facilities for efficient access, versioning, commenting, confidentiality, and security.

How can effective systems of this type be developed? After reviewing the CSCW literature we believe that two crucial areas have not yet received sufficient attention.

The first area concerns the analysis of user requirements. Most existing CSCW tools have been developed in order to try out a new technical idea, such as the use of semi-structured messages or of graphs that represent possible speech-act sequences. In this approach the tool is developed first, and possible uses are sought afterwards. When launching a new technology such an approach may be inevitable: people did not realize that they needed Walkman cassette players until Sony produced them. However, for large-scale commercial applications we believe that necessity should be the mother of invention: before designing what will inevitably be a very large and complex system, the work context in which the system will be used should be carefully studied. Lip service is often paid to this principle, but in practice the amount of time and energy devoted to studying user requirements is usually tiny in relation to the whole project. To correct this inbalance we need not only a change of attitude, but also a repertory of concepts and procedures for modelling enterprises. Even when system designers recognize the importance of analysing user requirements, they may neglect this task simply because they lack clear ideas on how to proceed. For this reason, one of our main aims in the present project has been to develop a methodology for modelling cooperative enterprises.

The second area in need of greater attention is that of integration. All CSCW applications include some basic functions such as the storage and display of documents. If these functions are implemented separately for each tool, then when tools are linked into a more complex system many functions will be duplicated, and special interfaces will have to be built so that documents produced by one application can be read by another. To avoid this inconvenience and wasted effort, we believe that CSCW tools should be developed with reference to a common environment which includes all shared functionalities such as the user interface and the management of documents. After such an environment has been built, any new CSCW tool can be developed much more quickly, and integration with existing tools becomes virtually automatic. Another main aim of this project has been to define a general architecture for CSCW systems, and to specify the functions which should be provided by the shared environment.

3 The case studies

Paolo Amadio, Ilario Fassina

1. The high speed train

1.1 Context

FIAT EMMEPI provides consultancy in project management. From the projects recently undertaken by the company, we selected as most relevant the construction of the ETR 500 high-speed train for the Italian railway.

The Italian state railway is called "Ferrovie dello Stato" (FS). During 1985 the FS decided to build a new high-speed train, the ETR 500, capable of running at over 300 km/hour on a straight track. They intended to finish two convoys by May 1990 so that they could make their debut during the world cup. The work was subcontracted to a group of four companies, one of which was made responsible for coordination. This system did not work properly since the coordinator was assigned two conflicting roles, and the project went out of control by mid-1988 when the first prototype was almost completed and the construction of the two complete convoys had just started.

A great deal of the work of coordination had to be undertaken by the FS, or more precisely by a section of the FS called the "Direzione Centrale Materiale Rotabile" (DCMR). However, although the DCMR had a good project manager, and good design and testing offices, it was not equipped to ensure the progress control needed in such a project, so in October 1988 this task of coordination support was assigned by the DCMR to EMMEPI. Under this regime the construction of the convoys proceeded until June 1990, when one convoy was ready for use during the world cup in demonstration trips with reporters and politicians. The train is now operating regularly twice a week between Florence and Rome for a final test, and the FS has decided to put 30 complete convoys into production.

When EMMEPI began monitoring the project, it had to deal with the following difficulties.

(a) Although a prototype for the ETR 500 had been built, the final product required further technological innovation.

(b) Compared with similar projects abroad, the time allotted was very short.

(c) Neither the DCMR nor the group of constructors (the four companies) had a planning-control system capable of supporting the management of the project.

(d) As a result, no overall work plan or information service had yet been created.

(e) The constructor companies were dispersed over several different cities in North Italy; one was also located at Naples.

The operational conditions could be classified as follows (see section 3): the task was non-repetitive; the product specifications and coordination procedures were indeterminate; and there were many interacting concurrent subtasks. In such a situation, the cooperative style of management is a plausible approach.

1.2 Measures adopted

When managing a construction project, two documents must be maintained: a product specification, and a work plan. For established products, built by established methods, these documents can be written in definitive form at the beginning of the project. When this is possible, the project is said to be deterministic, or mechanical, or closed. For innovative products such as the high-speed train, the exact form of the final product and the work plan cannot be forseen; therefore the original documents must be revised constantly as the work proceeds.

Before starting to build the two convoys, the FS and the constructor companies had to define the design of the train in detail. As mentioned above, some important technical innovations were required in respect of the prototype ETRX500, but the main problem lay not only in the new product specification but also in the work plan.

To create a realistic work plan, consensus had to be reached on issues like the division of the work into subtasks, how each task depended on others, and how long each task should take. This consensus did not exist. Each company had prepared a plan for its own portion of the work, but these plans reflected the needs of individual companies rather than those of the whole project. Consequently, although some subtasks were performed, overall temporal coordination was absent. Reports and estimates from the constructor companies were distorted through fear of losing face, or fear that a task might be reassigned to a competitor.

To correct this situation, EMMEPI used two strategies. First of all, they oriented the FS and the constructor companies to give more emphasis to achieving the common objective and less to pursuing sectional interests. Secondly, they provided support in the form of an information service, maintaining an integrated picture of current progress, and informing each company of relevant developments at other sites. These general aims were achieved by the following measures.

(a) A coordinating committee was established, comprising the project managers of the constructor companies, the project manager of the DCMR, and EMMEPI.

(b) A common language for the project was agreed, to prevent misunderstandings over essential technical terms.

(c) The existing work plans of each company were collected, and shown to be inconsistent with the project guidelines owing to problems of temporal coordination.

(d) EMMEPI applied pressure on the coordinating committee to formulate a single coherent work plan. (There is a story that the company representatives were locked in a meeting room and not allowed to leave until they had reached agreement.)

(e) A detailed version of the plan, including 2500 subtasks, was created with standard PERT/CPM software.

(f) Special forms were drawn up for reporting progress and future estimates. These forms had to be compiled each week by DCMR observers, who were already present in each factory to check that technical specifications were being correctly followed.

(g) To prevent delays, a weekly timetable was set up to regulate the frequency and speed of reporting and verification, so that for example a report on the situation on Friday would be distributed to project managers by the following Tuesday.

(h) For each activity, "necessary" and "possible" dates had to be entered in the relevant form. The necessary date specified when the activity should be finished in order to avoid delaying the overall plan. The possible date estimated when the company would really be able to finish, in view of the progress achieved so far.

(i) By integrating information from these reports EMMEPI maintained a "compatibility picture", which showed how delays in supplying components would affect plans for assembly. In this way, critical situations were identified.

(j) Critical situations were resolved by negotiation among the project managers. If a component needed for assembly was delayed, then the assembly date was changed, or parts of the production task were assigned to other sites. For issues that could not be settled by direct negotiations among project managers, a monthly coordination meeting was convened.

Different methods were adopted to avoid the disruption of critical activities by delays elsewhere. In some cases for example a simulation maquette was delivered instead of the real component. The maquette would enable work to continue on preparing routes for cables and other connections. Where possible, likely sources of disrpution were anticipated and contingency plans were drawn up.

As well as tackling the problem of misinformation, measures (f) and (h) provoked discussions within each company which helped to change their attitudes. As a rule, companies are unwilling to disclose information about their progress and about expected future disruptions. They prefer to admit responsibility only after the disruption has occurred.

Such conflicts of interest were observed on several occasions at the beginning of EMMEPI's involvement with the project. Having received no information from company technicians, the DCMR observers sent the EMMEPI planning technician their own estimates of work in progress and their own forecasts. These estimates, which were sometimes pessimistic, were passed on to the coordinating committee together with comments and complaints from the client and the suppliers. When this happened, the project manager of the company responsible for the delay usually sought out the responsible technician. Their conversation might have proceeded as follows.

PM: The DCMR inspector says that the component will arrive five weeks late. Is that true?

T: Well, we are a bit behind schedule ...

PM: You didn't have to tell him that. If they think we need so much time to make the component, they will hold us responsible for disruptions on other sites, not yet declared, which will now be attributed to our delay. You should have said we would deliver on time.

T: I said nothing. But he kept asking questions to the workers and looking at what we'd done so far. It never occurred to me that the DCMR controller would give such a false report to the client. In future I'll check all his reports personally. Anyway, the controller doesn't realize that we have taken some measures to reduce the delay to two weeks. Do you think this will still cause problems?

PM: It could be okay. Anyhow, in future don't allow any information to go out of here without checking it.

This kind of discussion inside and among companies improved the quality of negotiation, by providing more transparent and reliable information, and hence facilitated cooperation among the organisations involved. The broadening of participation in generating, communicating, and utilizing information for decision making was in our view the key factor in the eventual success of the project. The methods used here could be seen as representing, in embryonic form, a cooperative style of project management based on continuous negotiation among the participants.

1.3 Conclusion

The work plan was created and maintained by one of the standard project management programs. Such programs work well provided that they receive, as input, a true description of the tasks to be accomplished, together with realistic time estimates. For projects carried out by a single organization, compiling this description might be straightforward. But when several organizations participate, we no longer have a single reliable source of information, but instead a debate among conflicting viewpoints. Before creating a work plan, these differences must be resolved, by discussion and negotiation, into a single coherent definition of tasks and constraints. Such a discussion could be supported by a CSCW system allowing users at remote locations to put forward views on each topic, to comment on the views of others, and to modify their positions during bargaining and mediation.

2. Environmental protection

2.1 Objectives

Lombardia Informatica is a Milan-based company which develops information technology applications for public administration, especially for the Lombardy regional authority. The project studied here has the objective of creating a unified information system for environmental control in Lombardy. It is funded by the Italian Ministry for the Environment. This project was judged interesting in the context of CSCW because it requires cooperation among many organisations, most of which are public bodies.

The protection of the environment can be divided into two main tasks: monitoring and intervention. The basic resources of air, water, and land must be checked constantly to ensure that they are not poisoned by industrial wastes or emissions; if a sudden crisis occurs, or if an unfavourable long-term trend is identified, then appropriate measures must be taken. Both in monitoring and intervention, responsibility is spread among many authorities, distinguished partly by geographical scope, partly by administrative level, and partly by technical field (e.g. air, water, solid waste). In the past, each of these organisations has built up its own information system, without reference to a common plan, and without any significant attempt to exchange and integrate information with other related organisations. Thus facts which could be usefully combined may reside in separate databases, so that they never come to the attention of the same person; or two organisations may base their actions on contradictory information, without realizing the inconsistency and trying to clear it up.

Although the objective of unifying the information system is obviously important, the realization of this objective has proved exceedingly difficult, owing both to the complexity of the domain and to the different perspectives adopted by the various authorities.

2.2 Scope of the problem

As an initial step, the Lombardy regional authority suggested to the Ministry of the Environment that a unified system of quality control should be created for the basin of the river Lambro, an area currently classified as high risk. Even when delimited in this way, the scale of the problem remains immense, as the following statistics show.

The area is 3320 sq. kilometers.
There are three rivers: the Lambro, Olona, and Seveso.
There are four districts: Milan, Como, Varese, and Pavia.
381 municipalities must be taken into account:
- some are located in the basins of the three rivers mentioned above;
- others have waterways which naturally or artificially drain into the three rivers;
- others have underwater streams connected to the three rivers.

(Overall, the Lombardy region has 10000 water sources, 40000 wells, 5000 acqueducts, 5000 sewers, 2000 rivers, and 50 lakes.)

Over this geographical area, the system should make it possible to monitor pollution sources and their distribution, the level of utilization of water resources, the extent of land reclamation, and the quality of the air. The project allows the public administration to define the priorities of different environmental requirements, both present and future, in relation to the resources presently available. In designing the system, great attention has been paid to defining its purpose, its logic, and its technical concepts, in a manner not only coherent in itself but also compatible with the requirements of Government and other interested parties. It is intended that the system should rationalize these divergent competences, so that coordination is enhanced by moving towards a common perspective as well as by collecting together all relevant information in a single database.

2.3 Environmental protection agencies

Responsibility for environmental protection is distributed among a large number of organisations which can be grouped conveniently into three administrative levels. At the lowest level, operational interventions are carried out by the municipalities and by consortia of private companies. At an intermediate level, coordination and data gathering are carried out by the districts. Finally, at the highest level, programming and control are carried out by regional and central government.

To show the complexity of the problem, more details will now be given about the internal structure of these organizations.

Lombardy regional authority: the system is being developed with the support and funding of central government (the Ministry of the Environment); the owner of the system will be the Ecology and Environment Section of the Lombardy Regional Authority.

Within this section there are the following departments.

(i) The *General Affairs Bureau,* in collaboration with other departments, is responsible for: (a) Legislative initiatives.
- (b) Editing the daily reports from various departments and controlling approval procedures.
- (c) Processing reports on funds dedicated to environmental protection.
- (d) Cooperating on the regional development program.
- (e) Cooperating with the office for control and planning of projects.
- (f) Managing relations with external organisations.

(ii) The *Planning Bureau* is responsible for:
- (a) Cooperating with the planning offices for each area in the preparation of forecast reports.
- (b) Promoting specific investigations and documenting the results.
- (c) Collecting data and performing statistical analysis.

(iii) The *Air Protection Service* is responsible for:
- (a) Promoting and coordinating projects for collecting data on air pollution and for taking any technical or administrative measures that turn out to be necessary.
- (b) Processing meteorological analysis that is related to air pollution in cities or on industrial zones.
- (c) Planning emergency interventions in severe cases of air pollution.
- (d) Organising records on emissions into the air.
- (e) Promoting and controlling initiaitives concerning pollution control.

(iv) The *Water Care and Management Service* is responsible for:
- (a) Promoting and coordinating the collection of data concerning the regional water system, water maps, and the atlas of water supplies.

(b) Checking that technical and administrative procedures for treating sewage, managing sewers, and defending underwater springs, are carried out, and that disciplinary actions are enforced.

(c) Formulating plans for reclaiming water systems.

(d) Defining chemical or biological problems due to the use of dangerous substances.

(e) Checking that technical and administrative procedures are properly carried out in the payment of funds to municipalities for investing in purification machinery; enforcing disciplinary measures when necessary.

(v) The *Solid Waste and Industrial Mud Service* is responsible for:

(a) Checking that technical and administrative measures are properly carried out in the collection, transport, and disposal of urban solid waste.

(b) Drawing up plans for the disposal of domestic and industrial muds, and coordinating the related monitoring activities.

(c) Promoting research on the collection and disposal of all kinds of solid waste.

(d) Checking that in waste pollution emergencies, the correct technical and administrative measures are taken.

The districts: According to a new law introduced in June 1990, the Districts will have to establish and utilize a land plan which will go beyond existing planning responsibilities by defining general territorial assets. In particular, it will determine how each piece of land may be used, and will lay down guidelines for interventions on the water system, taking into account possible effects on geological structures, forests, and other land features.

2.4 Aspects of the system

As already mentioned, environmental protection is complicated by the need to involve different public and private organisations. In the planning and implementation of a unified information system for the Lambro basin, the following organisations have been consulted while drawing up the functional specifications of the system.

(i) Three regional enterprises owned by the Lombardy Regional Authority.

(ii) Three private companies which, constituted as a consortium, will carry out the project.

(iii) Many offices belonging to the Ecology Department.

(iv) Many regional offices of other departments.

(v) The Districts in the Lombardy region.

(vi) A consortium of the relevant municipalities.

When the system is installed, several different organisation will have to participate in managing it:

(i) The Lombardy Regional Authority, and in particular various services in the Ecology department.
(ii) The Districts, which will coordinate data collection and monitoring.
(iii) Lombardia Informatica, which will manage and maintain the system.
(iv) Local health care units, which will be responsible for reporting on sanitation.

It follows that cooperation among different organisations will be necessary not only during the development of the information system, but also after it is installed.

2.5 The problem of coordination

As a more detailed example of the way in which many organisations must collaborate in order to manage and protect environmental resources, we will focus on the particular case of water. This can be regarded in various perspectives:

(i) As an environmental resource;
(ii) As an economic resource;
(iii) In relation to the land;
(iv) In relation to its quality;
(v) In relation to the weather.

Different departments adopt different perspectives, which lead in turn to different questions. For instance, from an economic point of view we can distinguish:

(i) Drinking water;
(ii) Mineral content;
(iii) Water power;
(iv) Irrigation;
(v) Industrial uses;
(vi) Outlets for waste;
(vii) Navigation.

For *drinking water*, the relevant organisations are the Health Department, which is concerned with quality, the Civil Engineering Department, which is concerned with the catchment basin, and the Ecological Department of the Regional Authority (as well as some District offices) which have to maintain census records.

Minerals in water are the concern of the above organisations and also the Industry Department.

Responsibility for *waste* is divided between the Health Department and the Districts.

Navigational aspects are dealt with by the Transport Department.

For *irrigation*, responsibility is shared by the Agricultural Department, the consortium of municipalities, and the Civil Engineering Department.

In a word, our problem is that of coordinating these numerous and diverse activities and organizations by means of suitable behavioural procedures and technological supports, in the context of a unified information system.

3. User requirements for CSCW

3.1 Cooperation and coordination

Manufacturing and service industries are becoming increasingly complex as they demand more specialized technologies and skills. To manage the work, many different people, competences, and viewpoints, must be coordinated.

Cooperation may be regarded as a method of achieving coordination. To decide whether cooperation is an appropriate method for a particular context, we must analyse how people and tasks are coordinated in that context.

Both in manufacturing and service industries, coordination is usually easy when the work is repetitive. In such cases, coordination can be supported by well-defined processes and procedures which will require little modification as the work proceeds (e.g. in mass production).

Coordination becomes more difficult when the same resource may contribute to several lines of production. However, more complex processes and procedures (flexible production) can still be defined. Methods of coordination are relatively specific and stable; they could in principle be performed by an expert system.

For non-repetitive activities, like projects, coordination can no longer be accomplished by a stable procedure. Even though the products, objectives, and major constraints, are defined in advance, the processes and procedures originally planned usually have to be modified during operation.

When coordination becomes harder, owing to greater complexity, a common reaction is to increase the size, scope, and power of the agency responsible for coordination (see matricial organizations). This policy leads to more bureaucracy and higher cost, but does not achieve any significant improvement in the effectiveness of coordination. It seems that beyond a certain level of operational complexity, a different approach is needed.

3.2 Complexity

To investigate whether there are domains of complexity for which traditional approaches do not work properly, two components of complexity can be distinguished:

(i) *Contemporaneity:* This means that several interdependent actions are performed at the same time - or almost the same time. Various situations of this kind may occur:
  - The actions could be performed at the same place or at different places;
  - They could be performed by the same people or by different people;
  - These people could have different levels of interdependence (different departments of the same company, or different companies playing different roles such as supplier, client, partner, shareholder).

Contemporaneity arises because competition squeezes the time available to complete the work (time competition).

(ii) *Unpredictability:* This means the details of the work plan and product specification cannot be stated definitively in advance, because there are many ways of accomplishing each task, and it is not certain which way will prove best. In such conditions, the balance shifts towards non-repetitive activities as opposed to repetitive ones.

If for each of these two factors (contemporaneity and unpredictability) we distinguish two levels (low and high), we obtain four possible domains of complexity (figure 3.1).

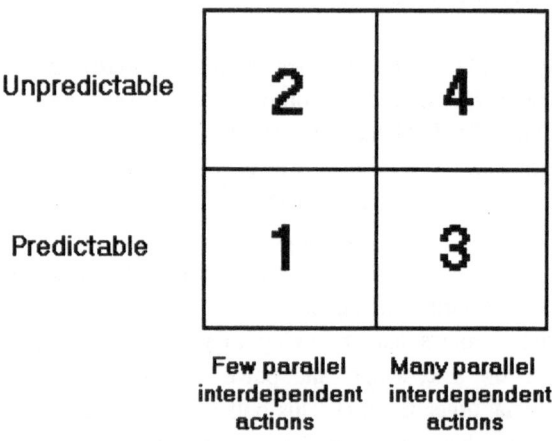

Figure 3.1 Four domains of complexity

With reference to the conditions under which decisions are taken (management actions), the four domains can be described as follows.

Domain 1: Not critical. There is sufficient time; definite procedures are available.

Domain 2: Competence is critical. There is sufficient time, but no definite procedures, so the best path must be chosen.

Domain 3: Time is critical. Definite procedures are available, but time is short.

Domain 4: Time and competence are critical. Time is short, and no definite procedures are available.

Some structural *solutions* to these conditions are shown by figure 3.2, in which cooperation is considered to be the answer to the fourth domain of complexity.

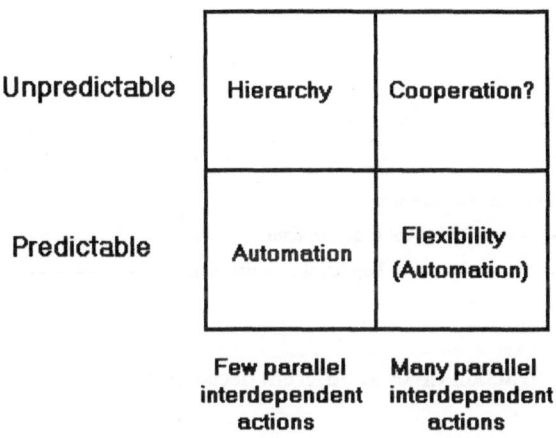

Figure 3.2 Solutions for the four complexity domains

In searching for appropriate solutions for the fourth domain, the following implications of high contemporaneity and unpredictability should be considered.

(i) Contemporaneity (time is critical): What typically occurs is that the procedures in force are too slow to resolve unexpected problems effectively.

(ii) Unpredictability (competence is critical): The unpredictability may concern *objectives* (product specifications, results to be achieved, issues, etc.), or *actions* (the work plan), or *people* (their roles and responsibilities), or *relationships* among these aspects.

Figure 3.3 shows how the cycle "Problem identification - Communication - Decision - Action" is enacted in a hierarchical structure with three levels. Note that problems requiring a solution in less than six time periods cannot be passed up to the top level (assuming normal procedures and timing) because the decision would arrive too late.

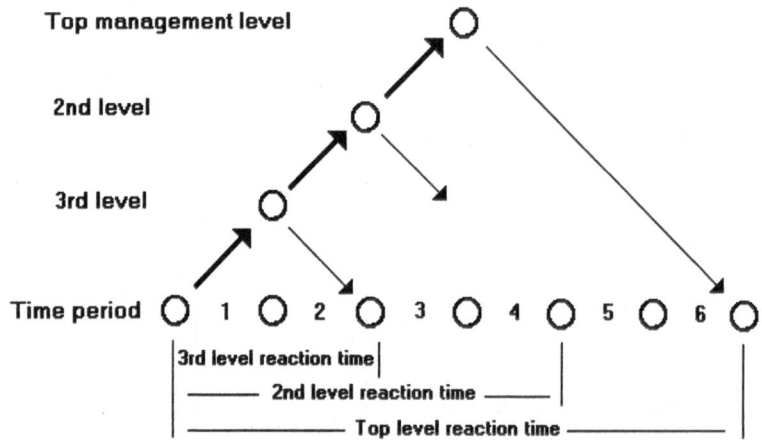

Figure 3.3 Reaction times at different decision levels

Since the appropriate response to unpredictability depends upon the required reaction time, it is important to investigate this issue when deciding how to achieve effective coordination. The total reaction time will increase if more than one organization is involved.

When the required reaction time becomes shorter and shorter, there may be no way of speeding up procedures without endangering decision quality. In such cases two solutions should be adopted: first, the number of hierarchical levels contributing to the decision should be reduced; second, direct lines of communication should be established between the relevant people. The latter solution could be facilitated by CSCW technology.

This method of coordination is based on the reference model of *negotiation*, rather than the traditional decide-order-execute model. Support for negotiation is needed at all moments of the management cycle (planning, action, verification, correction). In the cooperative approach the entire activity is regarded as a combined multiple supplier-client network.

3.3 Project management and CSCW

Projects are an example of non-repetitive activities. In project management, questions of coordination are essential since disperate people and resources are brought together specifically for the project, and must work together efficiently straight away, since they will not get a second chance. Several coordination methodologies and computer tools have been developed for project management; these may prove an interesting basis for CSCW systems.

Some common types of project can be classified, using the four domains of complexity, as follows.

(i) Environmental, medical, and research projects are of type 2 since they maintain the sequence "Theory - Study - Experiment - Design - Implement", and safety is more important than time.

(ii) Factories, complex buildings, petrochemical installations, and productive investments in general, are of type 3 because time is of fundamental importance and the objectives, agents, and action specifications, even if complex, are defined clearly at the outset.

(iii) Novel products and organizational changes are of type 4 since although the overall objectives and time limits are defined, the detailed specifications and work plan have to be progressively modified as work proceeds.

This classification is of course only approximate. In reality it might happen that two different projects in the same field, or even two parts of the same project, belonged to different complexity domains. Thus in some cases different management approaches will coexist, and should not be considered in conflict.

In fact, some basic methodologies such as the management cycle (plan, act, verify, correct) remain similar across the different approaches. In domains 2 and 3, the management cycle can be realized hierarchically, so that the people who plan, verify, and correct, may be different from those who act (the executors).

The hierarchical approach implies a separation of executors from the other roles. Executors are tied to a rigid predetermined plan of operations, and they have no duties other than complying with this plan. Although changes to the plan are admitted in principle, they are discouraged in practice. When events do not go according to plan, the plan is considered correct and what actually happened is considered wrong.

The difference between the support systems needed in domains 2 and 3 are due mostly to the difference in the required reaction time, which is shorter in 3 than in 2.

In domain 4, the same management cycle has to be realized by all participants, each being aware of the whole task. Consensus among the participants about the work plan is more important than the completeness and precision of this plan; any necessary adjustments will be agreed later depending on how matters evolve. Coordination is achieved not by defining all activities precisely at the outset, but by remaining closely in touch so that problems can be tackled as they arise. As well as executing his own task, each partcipant should take part in defining the plan, monitoring and reporting his own progress, studying reports about the progress of others, evaluating the consequences, making any necessary adjustments in his own operations, requesting corrective action from others, and negotiating changes to the agreed plan.

3.4 CSCW system requirements

As a working hypothesis we may assume that the shift from a hierarchical approach to a cooperative approach does not alter the fundamental tasks of management, nor the related methodologies. Rather than abandoning standard methods, we should supplement them by the further functionalities that are needed for the cooperative approach, in which each participant may play a wider role.

Thus when designing a CSCW system, we should start from the existing coordination methodologies and computer tools (which have been created with reference to the hierarchical model) and add the facilities deriving from the cooperative (negotiation) model. Such a system would have the advantage of incorporating, as a special case, the functions related to the hierarchical model.

4 Modelling the case studies

Mike Martin, Graeme Oswald

1. An approach to enterprise modelling

1.1 What is enterprise modelling?

The current state of the art in representing organisations emphasises that division of labour is a common denominator of all organisations. The "primary tasks" (Rice 1958) of enterprises are divided into smaller, more manageable tasks. The sub-tasks and their relationships give rise to information needs and information flows, and it is these features which define functionality requirements. Consequently, traditional systems analysis techniques concentrate upon capturing these aspects of organisational life. Division of labour is not, however, only concerned with the division of tasks. This division also produces differential responsibilities. The division of responsibilities produces different work roles which staff occupy. Each work role defines the responsibilities laid upon the role holder, the relationships with related roles, and the expectations imposed by related roles. The work role not only defines the task responsibilities, and therefore the functional requirements, but also the rights and obligations of the role-holder, which helps to define many, if not all, of the so-called non-functional requirements. It is this additional incorporation of a work role analysis which is currently lacking, and which the enterprise modelling approach provides.

If we look at the pattern of activities and information flows in an organisation, we are usually observing the results of an evolutionary process. This process is one of identifying activities and the resources they use on the one hand and defining responsibilities and obligations on the other. Both these aspects of organisations are important and policies and requirements range over both with equal significance. One of the main consequences of working in a conceptual framework which admits only activity and information is that policies about the allocation of responsibility and obligation must remain implicit.

The method of enterprise modelling has been developed to provide a rich enough conceptual framework to allow these issues to be expressed and analysed, yet one that is still simple and well structured enough to remain tractable. It has proved its usefulness in the following areas:

(i) The representation of aspects of organisational structure and policy particularly relevant to the issues of development and change.

(ii) The definition of requirements on information and communications systems to meet organisational requirements.

(iii) The analysis of the internal structures of organisations to identify opportunities for and consequences of splitting off units and functions as independent concerns. This involves the mapping of different variants of client - server relationships onto some form of consumer - provider relationship.

(iv) The evaluation of threat and vulnerability at the organisational level in the context of security and safety critical operations. This encompasses the breakdown of responsibility and obligation as well as failure of communication or function.

1.2 The components

The following sections describe the components from which an Enterprise Model is constructed. As with any modelling approach, there is an initial problem with terms. Within the method they acquire specific and precise meanings which sometimes do not accord with common practice. The alternative of inventing new terms adds to the problem rather than the solution.

Agents: An agent is an abstract concept. It is an entity which can be a party to a conversation with another agent resulting in the creation and discharge of mutual commitments. Such conversations involve agents generating and interpreting information. One of the distinguishing features of agents is that they are capable of initiating behaviour, without the need for any external stimulus: they have intent.

In the most abstract enterprise models, the agents are collections of obligations and responsibilities. These may be composed together or decomposed and structured to define roles for individual people, organisational units and whole enterprises in the more concrete models. By this process, the division of activity and resources and the allocation of responsibility and obligation within organisations and markets can be represented and analysed.

There is a finite set of relationships which can exist between two agents. One of these is consumer-provider which, by definition, exists between agents acting in their individual interests in the context of a market. It is presented in detail elsewhere in this report. The underlying analysis which allows us to distinguish between different types and instances of these relationships is based upon the nature of the conversations which they can have. These conversations are defined in terms of sequences of a basic set of primitive interactions which are interpreted as acts, that is to say, they change the state of obligation which the participants believe they have to each other.

If the interpretations of the participating agents do not correspond then that particular conversation has been defective. This may be due to an error of communication between the parties, an error of interpretation of correctly executed communications or to one of the parties reneging on an obligation. In any of these events, the parties need evidence or records of the conversation that has taken place. The items of evidence refer to the instruments of a conversation. They may take any of the following forms:

(i) Information resources such as documents and records together with a description of the context in which they were generated and interpreted;

(ii) Physical objects in their guise as products;

(iii) A report of the behaviour of a person or system, for example, " We shook hands" or "The 'accept' button was pressed on this terminal while you were logged on".

Access modes and access rights: There are two sorts of relationships between agents and resources. The first set we call access modes. These are the physical actions which an agent may perform on or with a resource. For example, an agent can create, destroy, read, write and modify information. She may also produce and consume physical resources. The second set we call access rights. These are the permissions and capabilities which an agent has over a resource. Typical forms are the right to generate and interpret information, to allocate and withdraw objects and to own or control facilities. A right associates an agent and resource with a particular conversation and these together represent the context in which particular access modes are executed. For an enterprise model to be well formed, each instance of an access mode upon a resource must have an explicit context, labelled as a conversation, which defines the allowed and intended interpretations of the action.

One quite complex but familiar example of modes and contexts is the interpretation of "off hook" executed by the called party in a normal telephone call. In the context of the conversation between the service provider and the calling party, the interpretation is a commitment of the latter to pay for the call. In the context of the conversation between the caller and the called party, the obligation is for the called party to confirm the called number.

The parties may not be thinking these interpretations each time they make a telephone call but they need to understand them if they are to be rational and competent subscribers. Anyone who is building a telephone system or an answering machine requires an understanding of the interpretations as well as the physical actions for the design to be effective.

2. The high speed train project

2.1 Introduction

One of the features of enterprise modelling, which is particularly useful in this study, is its ability to support the separate modelling of different aspects or views of an enterprise and then to allow the consequences of the composition of the different views into a single model to be examined. Since the different views represent different concerns, policies and issues, their combination reveals the possibilities for conflict and thus locates and defines contexts in which co-operative processes are required for the effective operation of the enterprise.

Before developing the models, we will examine those attributes of this case study which distinguish it from conventional industrial practice and which call for a distinctively co-operative approach. In discussions with the problem owner - representing the organisation which undertook the project management and co-ordination - the following factors, which are not presented in any particular order, were identified as of special significance.

The uncertainty associated with industrial innovation. This was clearly regarded as a critical factor which made conventional approaches to management planning and the implementation of quality systems inappropriate. In relation to the enterprise models, the consequence is clear: a simple mapping of responsibilities on to distinct individual roles, resulting in a rigid and inflexible structure, would almost always be defective. A commitment to the overall project called for a high degree of self-management and direction from the participants.

The clear criterion for failure. The approach of the world cup event and the need to demonstrate the train at that time gave a clear and unambiguous criterion for success or failure.

The enterprise was inherently distributed. The participation of different organisations throughout Italy and with wider European involvement presented specific communications and distribution constraints.

Non-explicit policy cannot be avoided. While the explicit objectives of the enterprise were, as indicated above, very clear, each of the participants maintained individual policies and interests which conditioned their relationships and behaviour. Any approach to structuring the organisation or to providing systems and services to support it cannot ignore this fact of life.

One key factor, which was judged to have contributed to the successful completion of the project, concerns the co-ordinating organisation's ability to identify and manage the consequences of changes in delivery schedules. Such changes happen in a local context but may have global consequences. They each involve negotiation between the directly concerned parties but also require the participation of an agency which protects the wider interest and which identifies and resolves, through mediation, the side effects of individual changes.

In this context, the model of co-operative structure and process represents, at its highest level, a complex web of commitments to deliver a project component. Each participating agent is dependent on a chain of supply, both direct and indirect. Each has a set of agents who are dependent on the appropriate and timely discharge of its own obligations. Our models must be capable of representing this network and allow us to reason about the effectiveness of methods for mediating and managing changes in its structure and operation.

The Italian high speed train project has been re-expressed in four initial sub-models.

(i) The operational model. This model is structured on the set of agencies which are the consequence of the concept of an engineering product life-cycle. Such agencies as *requirements analysis, design, build, test* and *commission* may be represented in this model. These agencies, in turn, may be structured into, for example, high level design, which defines the main sub-systems in terms of their interface and envelope, and detailed design which operates at sub-system level.

(ii) The management model. This represents the vertical structuring of the enterprise. A standard vertical model composed of *directing, managing* and *executing* agents will be applied to this case study but in doing so we do not imply that there are separate individuals who are directors making policy, managers making plans and executing agents who follow them. At this stage in the modelling process, the concept of agency is purely one of structuring responsibilities and obligations; the combination of agencies into roles for individuals and organisational units takes place at a later stage in the definition and description of an enterprise. As we will see, in an enterprise concerned with innovation, such as the one under consideration here, policy cannot be pre-formulated. Planning and execution interact constantly and responsibilites must be shared.

(iii) The business and commercial model. This model expresses the relationships between the *consortium members*, the *co-ordinating organisation*, the *client* - Italian railways - the *government*, which owns the client, and the *travelling public* who are the audience and putative beneficiaries of the exercise. Note that we are not claiming to be able to capture and formalise all the concerns and policies of these agencies. We must, however, identify them as separated domains of interest: they represent points of view from which any policy may be evaluated.

(iv) The model of co-operative structure and process. This is, of course, the most important model in the context of this study. The central concept around which the model is constructed is that of a decision conference: a number of stake holders - *participating agents* - who interact under the co-ordination of a *moderating agent* or chair person in order to achieve an objective in the form of a commitment. The model will also include a *sponsoring agent* who has the right to call the conference into existence and to set the terms of reference and an *implementing agent* who will be responsible for acting upon the decision.

The detailed definition of each of these models and the exhaustive evaluation of the ways in which they interact is far beyond the scope of this deliverable. Since our purpose is to define the requirements on the tools, services and systems needed to support the process of co-operation, a complete model is not required and we will concentrate on these specific aspects of the enterprise.

2.2 Overview of the models

The purpose of our models is to identify requirements on tools, information systems and services specifically to support a co-operation based style of management in large engineering projects. To specify requirements we must first characterise both the user of a tool and the context of its use. In the method we are exploiting here, users are defined in terms of the responsibilities and obligations that they have. The context of use of a tool is defined as the interpretation, in terms of the creation and discharge of these obligations, of operations on information resources. We do not limit ourselves to strictly functional issues - *what* the user needs to do - but also we wish to represent *why* it needs to be done and what, for example, the consequences of failure may be.

The management of consortia of independent organisations undertaking projects with a degree of innovation and uncertainty is the generic problem we address, and the solution we offer is a specific one. It involves the adoption of a particular style of organisational structure which is initially expressed in terms of a particular distribution of responsibilities amongst a set of organisational roles.

Within this concept, however, there is scope for variation of approach: the main dimension of variation will be the degree of centralised authority which can be asserted. There is no one ideal balance in this matter: it will depend on the policies and relative powers of the participants and may change at different stages in the lifetime of the co-operative enterprise.

In the following sections we present a brief description of each of the models in terms of the agents that they contain. The main difficulty encountered by those new to this modelling approach is to equate agents with individuals: this is incorrect. At this stage in the modelling process we have abstracted away from the assignment of agency to individual roles. In the next stage, when we start to combine the separate models of different aspects of the enterprise into a single model, we will construct roles for organisational units such as teams and individuals.

2.2.1 The horizontal model

The first model to be presented is referred to as a horizontal model. This term is used to refer to the structuring of the enterprise into mutually dependent units. The relationship between such units is an obligation to supply a component of the project to the user of that component by a required date and that the delivered item should be fit for its purpose. In the case of innovation, the criteria of fitness may not always be explicit. Three aspects of the enterprise figure in this model:

(i) The requirements definition, design, implementation and commissioning loop: a life-cycle concept;

(ii) The chains of suppliers and users starting with basic technologies, through components and sub-systems to systems;

(iii) The project co-ordination structure which provides global information for the optimisation of local provider - consumer transactions.

The model is based on a somewhat simplified and abstract view of the functional structuring of the organisation and of the product life-cycle.

Requirements and design: Expressed in enterprise modelling terms, the engineering life cycle in its simplest form calls for the definition of requirements by an *architect agent*, their interpretation by a *design agent* into executable designs which are, in turn, interpreted by an *implementing agent* who produces a product. This description does not imply a strict sequence; even in the domain of well understood systems and technologies, the process of refining the definition of requirements as part of the design and implementation process is inevitable. In the context of innovation, the process is essentially one of dialogue and negotiation between the needs and aspirations of the client and the constraints of technology and resources.

The greater the scope for dialogue, however, the greater the management uncertainty. One of the methods used in the HST project to control this problem was the splitting of design agency into high level design, which defined the major sub-systems in terms of their mechanical envelope and systems interfaces, and sub-system design which discharged design responsibility within these parameters. This results in clear demarcation and the ability to identify and localise the side effects of design changes while maximising local design freedom: an appropriate response to the uncertainty of industrial innovation.

Referring to figure 4.1, the client, architect and high level design agents together represent a domain of co-operation through shared responsibility. The groups of individuals who discharge these obligations will, at the next level of structuring of responsibilities, represent such issues as mechanical and electrical design, control systems, styling, safety, operational maintenance and many other individual engineering and design disciplines.

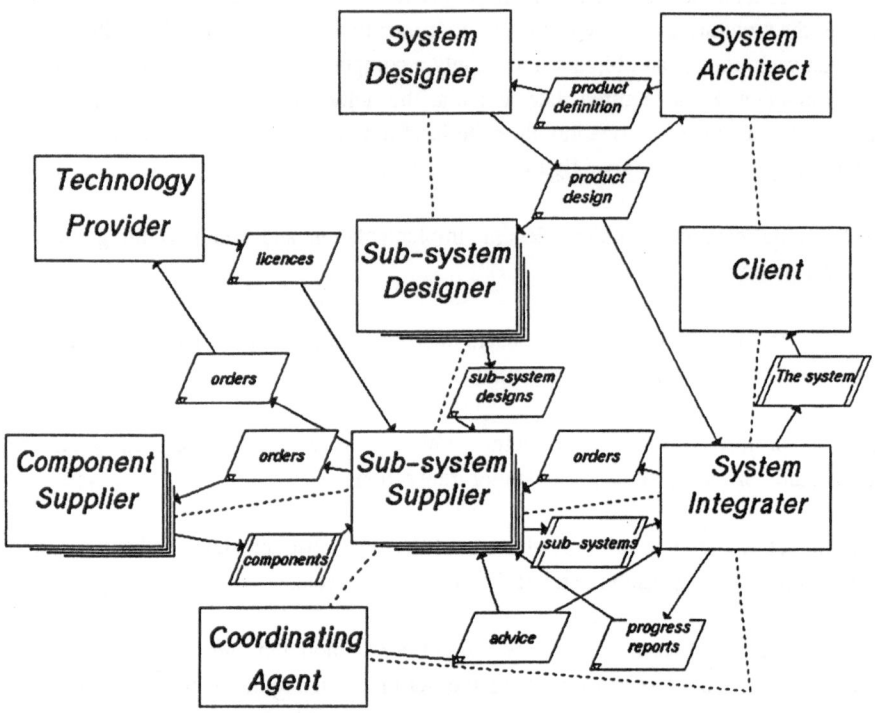

Figure 4.1 Horizontal model

Supply: The outcome of the design and the management planning processes is a set of tasks each of which is accepted as a commitment by one agent within the enterprise with respect to another agent. The commitment is defined in terms of the delivery of an item on or by a required date within the terms of a specification. For the purposes of structuring our model, we identify four classes of object as deliverables:

(i) Information objects, such as designs.

(ii) Systems and sub-systems which have been designed, built or tested.

(iii) Components which are distinguished from sub-systems in that, as far as the design of the product is concerned, they are merely specified or identified rather than designed. The design of a component remains the property of the supplier of that component.

(iv) Technologies which are delivered indirectly through components or sub-systems. Before a commitment is given to deliver either of these, the parties must be sure that the appropriate technologies are available. Where the discharge of the obligation to deliver involves innovation then the commitment should be two phased, the first to prove the capability the second to deliver the goods. A technology is not replicated and sold like a component or system but may be licensed by its owner.

The supply chain represented in the model links the *system integration agent* with a set of *sub-system supply agents*. Each of these, in turn, have a set of commitment links to *component supply agents*. Any of these agents may be dependent on commitments from *technology supply agents*. Each sub-system supply agent is dependent on a *sub-system design agent* to furnish the design of the sub-system and they are dependent on the *system design agent* described above.

One of the factors distinguishing these different classes of supplier is the nature of the transfer of ownership of both the deliverable itself and of the design to which it conforms. This will represent an important element in the collaboration agreement at the consortium level.

Co-ordination: The model, as indicated so far, results in a network of relationships representing mutual dependencies and commitments. Each is made on the assumption that all dependent obligations in the chain will be met in an appropriate and timely way. In reality, commitments sometimes fail by being late or unacceptable or by turning out to be impossible or impractical. Such failures require fixing at the correct level in the enterprise and the side effects managed through modification of related and dependent commitments. Clearly the earlier a potential failure is identified, the more likely it is that an efficient compensatory action can be identified and executed.

It is the responsibility of the co-ordinating agent to ensure that these aspects of project managements are effected in the overall interests of the project. The specific obligations areas follows.

(i) To detect and notify likely and actual failures in delivery within the project to all the relevant parties.

(ii) To ensure that overall corrective planning (by managing agents) takes place at the lowest appropriate level so that the consequences of changes do not propagate higher in the design authority structure than necessary.

(iii) To ensure that the re-negotiation of commitments takes into account the interests of the overall project by identifying and characterising the side effects of local changes.

Co-ordinating agency does not carry with it the right to re-plan; this is a managing agent's responsibility. It does carry the right to information on progress and prospects in any part of the enterprise. A noteworthy feature of the HST project is that the usual practice of combining co-ordination and management agencies into a manager's role, i.e. co-ordination through the management structure, was not followed but a separate role created. This was cited as a reason for the effectiveness of the co-ordination process.

2.2.2 The vertical model

This model is concerned with the chain of responsibilities encompassing the definition of objectives which are attainable, the allocation of the financial, intellectual and commercial resources needed to achieve the objectives, the detailed planning and monitoring of activities against the allocation of specific resources and plans and the rendering of appropriate accounts of resource consumption and outcomes. This model provides a generic decomposition of each of the enterprise objects which figure in the horizontal model. For example, a design agent executes a set of design activities which are managed and directed.

The model includes three agents, *directing, managing* and *executing*. The obligations of the managing agent are to ensure:

(i) That sufficient appropriate resources are allocated to the executing agent. This includes raw material, information and tools to satisfy the demands of a particular client agent.

(ii) That the value of these resources is within the budget set by the directing agent and conforms to the resourcing policy.

(iii) That an adequate plan for use of the resources to achieve policy is produced.

(iv) That an adequate account for the operational use of the allocated resources is rendered and interpreted, e.g. to identify potential delays etc.

(v) That an adequate budgetary account is rendered. This is interpreted by the directing agent.

The management model is presented in figure 4.2.

The *directing agent* writes the policy, allocates the budget and interprets the budgetary account. These resource access modes are undertaken in the context of a director - executive relationship with the managing agent.

It is the right of the directing agent to decide objectives and to formulate policy to achieve them. These objectives must be achievable with the resources allocated, if they turn out not to be then this is a fault of direction.

The *executing agent* uses the tools, information and raw materials, in conformance with the plan, to produce the output. As with any agent who has resources allocated to them for a purpose, an account must be rendered.

The *consuming and supplying agents* may be regarded as having some version of a supplier - consumer relationship with the managed enterprise object. This is implemented in terms of orders or demands, payments, which may be notional within an enterprise, and the delivery of product. These relationships will figure in detail in the horizontal model. These agents equate to those in the horizontal model.

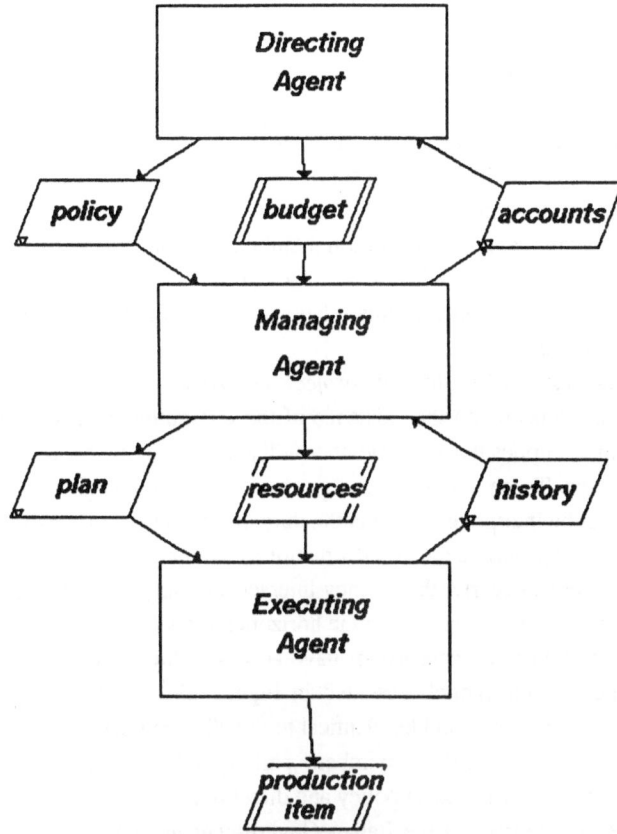

Figure 4.2 Vertical model

2.3 The business and commercial model

In this model we express the set of relationships and obligations associated with the concept of the HST consortium and its client, Italian Railways. The primary purpose of a consortium, from the point of view of the client, is that it simplifies a potentially complex set of contractual relationships into a simple one. The alternative for the client is to enter into a set of distinct contracts each of which may have to make reference to dependencies on multiple third parties. This approach is only appropriate for well understood, low risk ventures where component supply relationships are appropriate. The concept of the consortium internalises the mutual dependencies between the members. From the members' viewpoint, the consortium has the benefits of access and synergy at the cost of increased dependence on peers.

The conventional model of a consortium is structured on two classes of agents, a single prime contractor agent and a set of member agents. The model must also include the client agent.

The obligations existing between the client and the prime contracting agent are based, essentially, on one of supply, which has, as its instrument of commitment, an overall contract defining the objective of the transaction. This does not imply that the organisation having client agency cannot participate in other capacities within the consortium, for example, in design agency.

The prime contracting agent is structured into two agencies as far as the relationship between it and the consortium members are concerned. The first of these is the client management agent which acts as the contractual interface between the client and each of the member agents. In this relationship, the *client managing agent* acts on behalf of the members.

The second agency is that of *project co-ordination*. This is distinct from management and depends on the existence of the commitment of membership of the consortium which implies that each member will act in a way that will contribute to the common objective. To be able to discharge this obligation, the global implications of local events must be interpreted and it is the duty of the consortium co-ordinating agent to ensure that the appropriate global information is available to inform the decisions of consortium members. Clearly, this agency interacts strongly with management agency in the vertical model. It also appears in the horizontal model.

All agencies within the consortium have access to the contract and definition of objectives which, in the model presented in Figure 4.3, is generated by the project directing agent. This agent could be identical to the client enterprise or, as was the case in the HST project, consortium members participated in project direction agency allowing "bottom up" influence on policy and direction.

Figure 4.3 also represents the Italian Government in two roles, as owner of the railways and as civil authority in relation to the voting public. The latter, in the role of travellers, participates in a consumer supplier relationship with the railways.

The consortium members have pre-existing and independent relationships which need to be represented because they may be a source of conflict of interest. Thus, the consortium members already supply components, sub-systems and complete products to Italian railways. These are based on existing, well understood technologies and one of the motivations for participation is maintaining this domestic market. They also supply railway related products internationally and would wish to exploit developments from this project in those markets.

There will also be a set of external, component suppliers whose purchase contracts will figure in the internal dependencies of the consortium. It is a matter of policy whether the relationships with these suppliers are regarded as internal to consortium member organisations or a centralised purchasing function is operated on the consortium's behalf.

From the discussion of component and sub-system supplying agency, it is clear that a sub-system supplier must be a member of the consortium because of issues of ownership and agency over the design. If the provider maintains control over the design then the deliverable is a component by definition.

The situation with regard to technology provision is somewhat different. There is no fundamental reason why external technologies should not be licensed into the consortium. However, it is usually regarded as the criterion of a competent consortium that it owns or will develop all the specific technologies required for the project and that any externally supplied components used in the design will be available from multiple sources.

It is probable that the member enterprises regard some of their peers as competitors in some sectors. These issues are usually high on the agenda in the process of consortium formation and must be resolved at that stage. Clearly, the establishment and commitment to a common purpose is essential to the concept of a consortium.

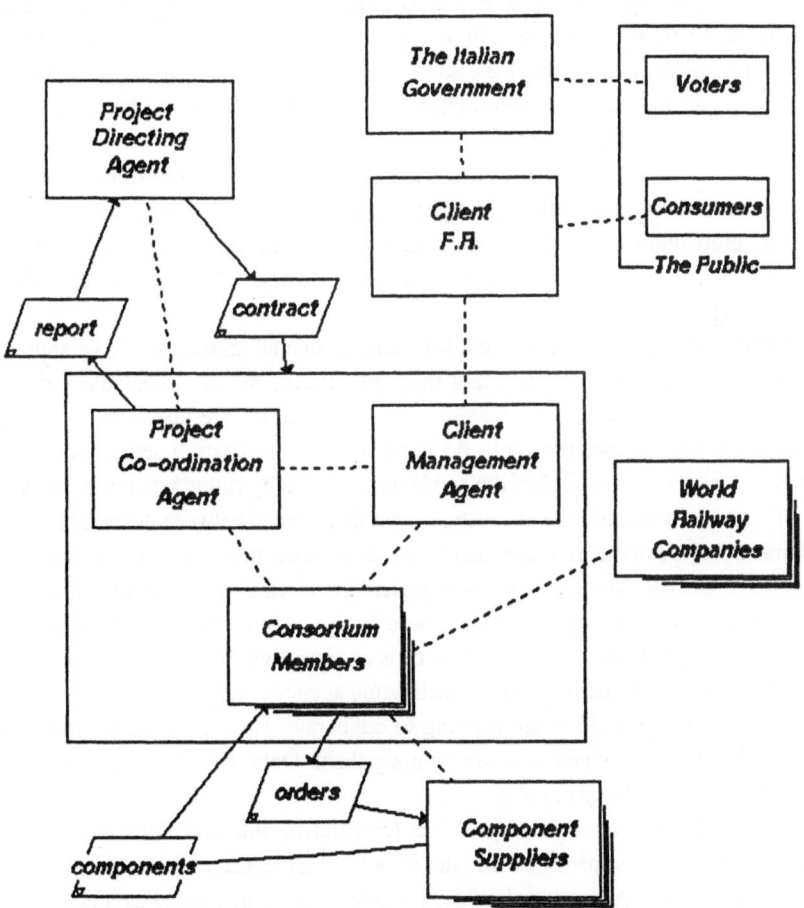

Figure 4.3 Consortium and commercial model

2.4 The decision conference model

We base the model of consortium co-operation on the concept of a decision conference. This provides the mechanism for a group of stake holders to come together to formulate a decision. Our model is composed of four types of agent, *sponsor, participant, moderator* and *implementer*. The moderator agent is structured into *chairing agent, facilitating agent* and *minuting agent*. Each of these agents will be described in terms of the obligations and responsibilities that they undertake.

The *sponsoring agent* has the right to call the decision conference into being, to invite and gain the commitment of the participating agents on the basis of a definition of the *terms of reference*. The sponsor will ratify the final outcome of the conference in the form of a *decision*.

The *implementing agent* has the responsibility to put the decision into effect. It is clear that for a conference to be effective, then the sponsoring agent must be able to grant the right and the resource to implement the decision to the implementing agent.

The *participating agents* commit to operating within the terms of reference and the rules of procedure. Participants have some sort of stake in the decision. It is part of the sponsor - participant dialogue to establish the interests which are to be represented by participation in the conference.

The *moderating agent* interprets the terms of reference and the submissions to the conference. This implies that if this agency is exercised by a number of different role holding individuals, then they are obliged to ensure that they have a common interpretation. As indicated above, the moderating agency is composed of the following three sub-agencies.

The *chairing agent* is responsible for ensuring that all participants have appropriate access to the conference process and that this process makes acceptable progress in accordance with the terms of reference. These obligations are discharged through the control of the conference protocol - deciding who has the floor or setting deadlines for submissions - and the control of the conference agenda by ruling what is in and what is out of order. It is through this mechanism that distinctions between definition of issues, statements of position and statements of consensus may be used to control the conference process. These categories represent interpretations of submissions. It is not the right of the chairing agent to make these interpretations, but is the joint right of the participating agents because the conference is co-operative. It is because of the need for such common interpretations that the facilitating agency is required.

[Note: Aborigine elders sit in a ring to deliberate. There is a special bone, from a wallaby I understand, which is passed among them. Only the elder with the bone may speak. Hence the "talking bone".]

The *facilitating agent* is responsible for offering interpretations and supporting analysis to the participants as an aid to achieving consensus of interpretation of submissions. In the case of a submission which is to be interpreted as a decision, then the nature of the analysis may take the form of the analysis of stated preferences or utilities.

The *minuting agent* is responsible for rendering the account of the deliberations and the decision to the sponsoring agent and to participants. The minutes are ratified on the basis of a consensus of the participants by the chairing agent. The latter is ratified by the sponsoring agent.

Figure 4.4 represents the model of the decision conference as described.

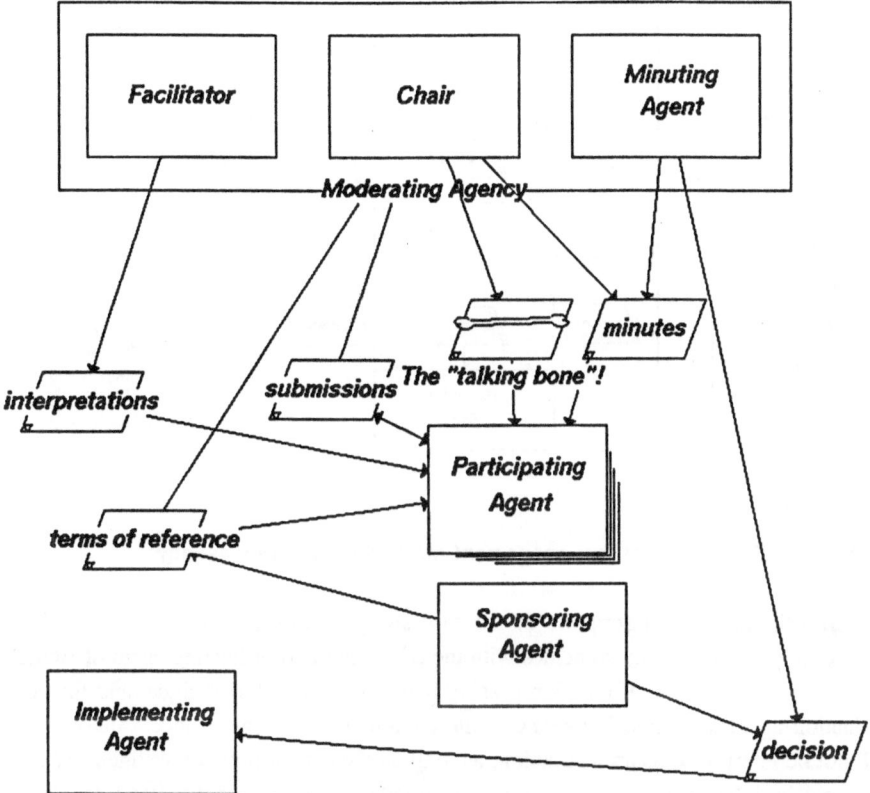

Figure 4.4 The decision conference

2.5 Issues of combining the models

It is not our intention to examine all the issues of the detailed combination of the models. We will concentrate in this case study on the problems of co-operative decision making and the roles of project co-ordination and the facilitation of decision conferences.

2.5.1 Combining the horizontal and vertical models

Each of the agencies identified in the horizontal models may be considered as a managed and directed enterprise object. Each of these objects will inherit a particular set of relationships with provider and consumer objects. They will also exhibit a relationship with a co-ordinating agent. Thus, in principle, each of the enterprise objects in figure 4.1, the horizontal model, could be replaced by a specific version of the model shown in figure 4.5.

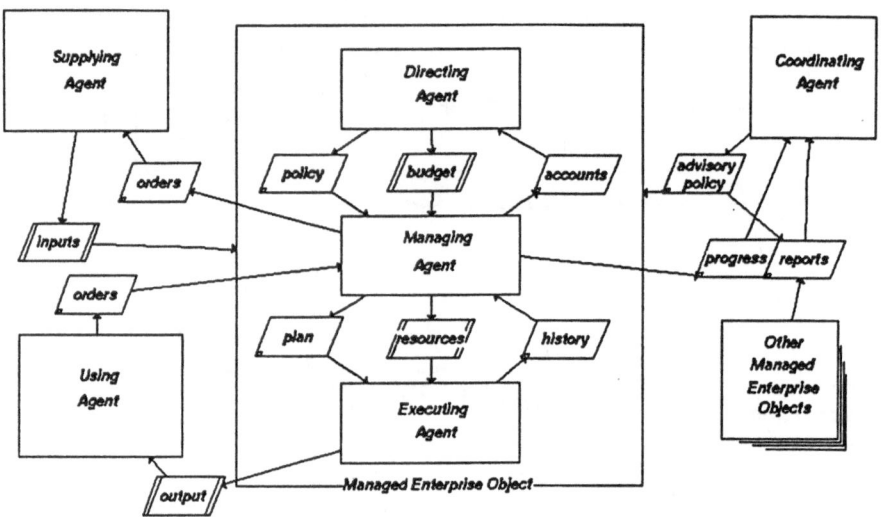

Figure 4.5 Applying the management model to horizontal agency

From the informal description of the case study it is clear that the co-ordinating agency shown in figure 4.5 coincides with the consortium co-ordinating agent of figure 4.3. To characterise the information passing between the enterprise object and the co-ordination agent as "advice" does not quite capture its true significance. Although it will not be interpreted as an instruction, as long as the consortium commitment exists, it should be interpreted as policy and be responded to as if in a director - manager conversation. With this in mind, we label this instrument as *advisory policy*.

2.5.2 Linking in the conference model

Given the evolution of the model of figure 4.5 we can distinguish two classes of conference: those that are internal to a managed enterprise object and those that take place between such objects. We will concentrate on the latter in this study. Since the conversations which can take place between these objects concern the establishment and discharge of obligations to deliver components of the project, this must be the subject of any conference.

Taking the model of figure 4.4 we can identify which agencies may be combined. The *sponsoring agent* for any particular conference could be any of the following:

(i) A providing agent (i.e. managed enterprise object) on the grounds that it wishes to re-negotiate a commitment which it believes it can no longer fulfil.

(ii) A consuming object on the grounds that a delivered item is not satisfactory or it wishes to re-negotiate the specification.

(iii) A co-ordinating agent on the basis that the parties to an existing commitment be subject to some side effect of other events in the project.

The *implementing agent* will usually be the provider in the commitment under negotiation.

Participating agents: the following agents would normally have a right to participate in a decision conference:

(i) The managing agents of the provider and consumer enterprise objects which are parties to the commitment under review.

(ii) The executing agents of the provider and consumer enterprise objects in the role of technical experts.

(iii) Other, directly affected enterprise objects. For example, the relevant design agent may be concerned in the negotiation between a sub-system supplier and a system integrator agent.

(iv) The co-ordinating agent has a special role as a participant in the conference in presenting the wider implications of the local decision.

The *moderating agency* should, ideally, be discharged by an individual who is viewed as independant and unbiased by the participants. This is not incompatible with co-originating agency.

The basis for representation at a decision conference is derived from an analysis of the model produced by combining the horizontal and vertical structures of the organisation. There is an orthogonal set of issues of representation at the conferences which is derived from the business and commercial model. These need to be combined with the principles already outlined to formulate the policy for participation.

2.5.3 Consortium issues

There are many practical justifications for ensuring that, wherever possible, the managed enterprise objects of figure 4.5 may be mapped onto teams who belong to individual consortium members. This reinforces the notion that the consequences of any particular outcome may be evaluated not only from the point of view of the overall project but in terms of the sectional interests of a particular consortium member as a commercial entity. The higher the level of the decision, the more vital and widespread are the interests that will be affected. Thus, the major project commitments will be negotiated at decision conferences where participation rights will be on a representative basis. Such conferences then become a means of implementing directing agency at the overall project level and we have the concept of a project board and management committee.

For co-ordination agency to remain compatible with conference moderating agency, it is necessary that the organisation undertaking the co-ordinating and client management role in the commercial model is limited to that specialised role. This accords with the experience of the case study where early problems were attributed to the fact that a consortium member also attempted to co-ordinate.

2.6 Requirements for tools and systems

Our intention is to specify a set of tools and facilities to promote and support the co-operative style of project management. It can be seen from the models we have presented that the two features of the enterprise which chiefly embody this approach are the concepts of co-ordinating agency and of the decision conference. If our tools are to be fit for their purpose then we must be able to demonstrate how they help these agents discharge their obligations more efficiently, with less risk of failure or with greater flexibility.

2.6.1 The co-ordinating agent's requirements

In the first instance we will assume that the responsibilities of co-ordination have been assigned to an individual who has no other responsibilites. This is in accordance with the principle that they should not, for example, be combined with management agency. This does not preclude the concept of a team of co-ordinators with an internal management structure; this would be represented as a decomposition of the co-ordinating agent in the consortium model and a redefinition of the co-ordinating agent as it appears in the horizontal model in terms of the sub-agencies.

The co-ordinating agent operates as an information broker, collecting, analysing, evaluating and selectively disseminating. There are three sorts of conversation relevant to this agency:
(i) The information gathering conversation with a managed enterprise object (see figure 4.5);
(ii) The presentation of advisory policy to such an object;
(iii) The presentation of overall progress reports at the consortium level.

Instances of the first sort of conversation are initiated at regular intervals by the information providing object, i.e. they are timetabled in the project planning and management framework. It is an obligation of the co-ordinating agent to ensure that all relevant information is included in any evaluation made. This implies that a reliable mechanism for identifying late or missing reports is available.

Instances of the second conversation are initiated by the co-ordinating agent as a result of analysing a set of reports. These conversations will usually result in the initiation of a decision conference which is, itself, costly. The quality of the decision to initiate such a conversation depends on the availability of all the relevant information and of the tools and resources to analyse and evaluate it.

Instances of the third sort of conversation are initiated on the basis of a timetable. The quality of the report is, again, dependent on the completeness and reliability of the input information and the correctness of the analysis to which it is subjected.

It is clear that a tool or system which may be depended upon to improve the completeness and reliability of the input data or to improve the capability to analyse and project from it will assist the effective discharge of co-ordination agency. We will refer to such tools as Coordination Support Tools (COST).

2.6.2 The information projection of COST

We will now examine the information resources which are relevant to the co-ordinating agent as a step toward defining the possible scope and functionality of the COST tools.

The instrument of an information collection conversation is a progress report. Each such report will be characterised by the following information items:

> The identity of the generating object
> A date of origination and sequence information
> The identity of the commitment in terms of:
>> The identity of the project component
>> The user of the component
>> The required date
>> The projected date
> The originator's estimate of confidence
> Corroborating evidence.

The interpretations required of each individual report are as follows:

(i) What is the level of confidence that can be attributed to it? i.e. what is the co-ordinating agent's estimate of the projected delivery date and the likelihood of acceptance?

(ii) Does it represent an actual or probable failure of obligation?

The previous reports of the reporting agent and the plans which are being executed are part of the context of this evaluation. It would also seem that some estimate is required of the complexity and novelty of the specific item being produced.

The second interpretation which the co-ordinating agent makes involves the evaluation of the report in the context of all the other current reports. It requires all the side effects of a failure to be explored and those that warrant re-negotiation to be identified.

2.6.3 Some initial issues of information integration and ownership

It is clear from an examination of figure 4.5 that the plan and the history which appear in the conversations between the managing agent and the executing agent refer to the same set of affairs as do the progress reports which are part of the managing agent - co-ordinator conversation. One of the most important policies that must be established is the level of information integration: Is it physically the same plan that the management agent writes for the executing agent and that is written for the co-ordinating agent. Is the executing agent engaging in two separate conversations when generating the history? The anecdote in the case study regarding the conflict between the technician, the manager and the DCMR inspector relate to this issue where the interests of the client and the project may be in conflict with the interests of an individual member.

Some issues of confidentiality will arise from the co-ordinating agent evaluation: this agent will not automatically accept the reporter's estimate of confidence but will apply a judgement based on past performance. Such an estimate is sensitive because on the one hand, the client is holding the co-ordinating agent responsible for the quality of the prediction but on the other, the subject may have a vital interest in a particular outcome.

It is important that we carefully define the range of confidentiality policies that our proposed tools will support and the basis upon which confidentiality may be relied. Thus, we may assume that the co-ordinated objects and the co-ordinating agents share a common system for reviewing progress and that there are no confidentiality domains: anyone may examine anything. At the other extreme, the co-ordinating system could be owned and accessed exclusively by the co-ordinating agent. Either of these positions represents a rational policy as do several intermediate positions. Do we intend to build a tool set that can be configured to support all or some or just one particular confidentiality policy ?

2.6.4 Functional overview

At this stage in the requirement definition process, we are able to embark on standard data and system modelling activities with a view to revisiting the issues of conversations and agency when evaluating the functional specification.

From the methodological point of view, we now identify the classes of information and communications systems and services which fit the general pattern of conversations and contexts we have identified. Clearly, the COST tools will be comprised of two components. The first of these will take the form of an information base which contains progress reports, accepts new reports and provides analysis and presentation functions to support the co-ordinator role.

The second component provides the means to define and populate a predictive model of the state of progress, both technically and in terms of project obligations, based on the state of the information base. The extent to which the product structure and design must be represented in this model in addition to the representation of the production process is not yet clear.

2.6.5 Supporting the decision conference

The second candidate for tools and systems to support the co-operative style of project management addresses the problem of implementing decision conferences.

Figure 4.4 is an extremely generic model. It does not commit to any policy of implementation or distribution. For example, the model fits a round table discussion, a video or voice conference or an E-mail conference. The events in the conversations identified in the model have certain rules of partial ordering but, within this constraint and those of the media of communications, may be distributed in time and space.

We can locate, in figure 4.4, the particular aspects of the conference which may be addressed with an information management tool or service. These are as follows.

(i) **The participation process**, which is under the control of the chair agent. The sort of support delivered in this area is directly dependent on the communications mode used to implement the conference. Much of the existing work in co-operative systems may be positioned here.

(ii) **The recording process**, which is the responsibility of the minuting agent, could be supported. In this area documentation systems are relevant but special emphasis must be placed on the patterns of shared ownership of the document. The information resource labelled "the decision" is the key product of the recording process but any tool which addresses the needs of a co-operative conference must pay particular attention to the complex life-cycle issues associated with the generation, refinement and final agreement to such a document. Clearly, the underlying document model is complex and related to a model of the conference process.

(iii) **The facilitation process**, which is responsible for ensuring the orderly and efficient progress of the conference process, is located in a particular agency in figure 4.4. Naturally, the individual who takes the role of chairperson must, necessarily, exercise some aspects of this agency. However, in our abstract model, we separate the responsibility to ensure that the process of participation is effective from the responsibility to ensure that the content of the participation is effective. Tools and systems to assist in this aspect of the conference could function as a participator group tool, a chairperson's tool or the tool of a specific user in the role of facilitator.

We discount tools to assist in the process of formulating terms of reference or implementing or monitoring the implementation of decisions in this discussion.

Each of the above areas for tool, system and service support warrants further examination. For the purposes of this study, however, we have singled out the issue of conference facilitation for further consideration because it is a relatively untried area for systems support and because it is highly relevant to the second case study we are undertaking.

2.6.6 The facilitation conversation

The facilitating agent has access to all submissions in the same way as a participant. The interpretation that the facilitator makes is, however, quite different from that of the participant. The facilitator may have the right to state the following with respect to submissions:

(i) The class of interpretation that appears to be appropriate. The system of classification is defined in a conference process model. This may include a view on whether a submission is out of order in relation to the terms of reference of the conference or out of order at this particular point in the conference.

(ii) That a submission implies certain consequences if it is adopted by the conference where the implications are outside the knowledge of the participants.

(iii) The areas of agreement and the areas of disagreement amongst the participants are thus and so....This may be applied to a state of consensus on a substantive issue or may apply to the interpretation of a submission.

These rights to interpret submissions raise a number of issues concerning the concept of the conference model. Initial discussions have proposed three classes of submission in a decision conference: the definition of an issue, the statement of positions and the presentation of an argument. It is not yet clear whether a dialogue structure or family of structures can be specified which characterise effective and efficient conferences. Such a specification would include protocols to ensure access and completion which are implemented through chairing agency as well as facilitation.

2.6.7 Issues in supporting the conference process

At this stage, a number of issues which are independent of the issues may be raised for further consideration and study. These are independent of the way that the conference is implemented in terms of media and distribution.

(i) What sort of assistance can be given in the process of categorisation of submissions? What scope is there for automation ?

(ii) Are the models and inference mechanisms required to assist consequence analysis in this context the same as those in COST ?

(iii) How far can such models themselves become the basis for the negotiation process with participants interacting through model parameters. Is there a game theory which would be applicable ?

(iv) While the network of project commitments looks, at least on the surface, to be both generic and tractable, how far can it be divorced from the model of the product itself which is, necessarily, specific.

3. The public administration case study

3.1 Introduction

This case study is concerned with a system for co-ordinating the operation of environmental protection agencies, district planning authorities and resource management agencies. The initial description of the problem has been presented in chapter 3. While a number of the issues in this case study are clear, it is, on the whole, less well characterised at this stage than the previous study. The models presented here must be regarded as provisional: a first attempt to explore the initial presentation of the problem.

We will introduce three models. The first represents the set of obligations which are discharged by an environmental protection agency and external agents with which it interacts. The second will present a local government planning and land management agency. This is an attempt to represent the new land use and planning legislation of the Lombardia region. The third model combines these two to explore the levels of integration which could, in theory, be achieved through shared ownership of information resources.

We have not attempted to represent the pre-existing distribution constraints of the Lombardia Region. In a more detailed study we would need to consider the fact that there are four, province based planning authorities, each containing many municipal authorities, that the responsibility for environmental protection is distributed between Air, Water and Solid Waste agencies and that there is a diverse set of resource management agencies such as navigation, power and irrigation. All of these have interests and obligations with respect to the environment and, thus, represent stake holders in decisions that affect its use and protection.

3.2 An environmental protection agency

The obligations placed on an environmental protection agency are as follows.

(i) To monitor the requisite set of environmental parameters from a specified, geographical area, maintaining records and providing access to the information to those who have a right to interpret it.

(ii) To analyse the environmental parameters in order to detect events or trends which are or would be injurious to the interests of beneficiaries of the environmental protection policy. These must be communicated to those who have a right or a need to know.

(iii) To formulate appropriate plans in response to injurious environmental events and trends.

(iv) To put the plans into effect in co-ordination with other agencies. This responsibility is split into two aspects:
- To instigate, undertake and co-ordinate physical interventions to improve, protect or remedy according to agency plans.
- To restrain external agencies from damaging activities and apprehending offenders, i.e. policing the environment.

These responsibilities map onto five internal agents within the generic model which is presented in Figure 4.6. The following paragraphs will describe each of the agents appearing in this model in terms of their conversations and information resources.

The *informing agent* is responsible for collecting and transmitting specific environmental data. This agent is not necessarily part of the protection agency. In the case study, there are instances of external organisations having a duty to compile regular reports on environmental quality for submission to an EPA.

The *monitoring agent* is responsible for the update and management of the set of environmental records which the EPA is required to maintain. If informing and monitoring agencies are assigend to different enterprises then the possibilities of a set of failures of transmission and interpretation are introduced.

The *evaluating agent* is responsible for the continuous interpretation of the totality of the environmental data. While criteria defining different classes of event are defined as part of the context of this evaluation, the obligation is one of care and the agent is responsible for detecting all threats that are identifiable within the state of the art.

Such obligations have associated with them the right to request specific, justifiable resources. If such requests are denied, then the evaluating agent may claim, before the event, that a certain class of threat may not be detected or responded to. This conversation takes place through the medium of the account and review relationship with the funding and directing agent.

The *beneficiary agent* represents individuals and organisations who are dependent on the quality of the environment and who rely on the funding agent to produce and implement an appropriate environmental protection policy. The relationship between the funding and the beneficiary agents is usually based on civil authority. The beneficiary agents have rights of access and quality, which are embodied in laws, with respect to the environment.

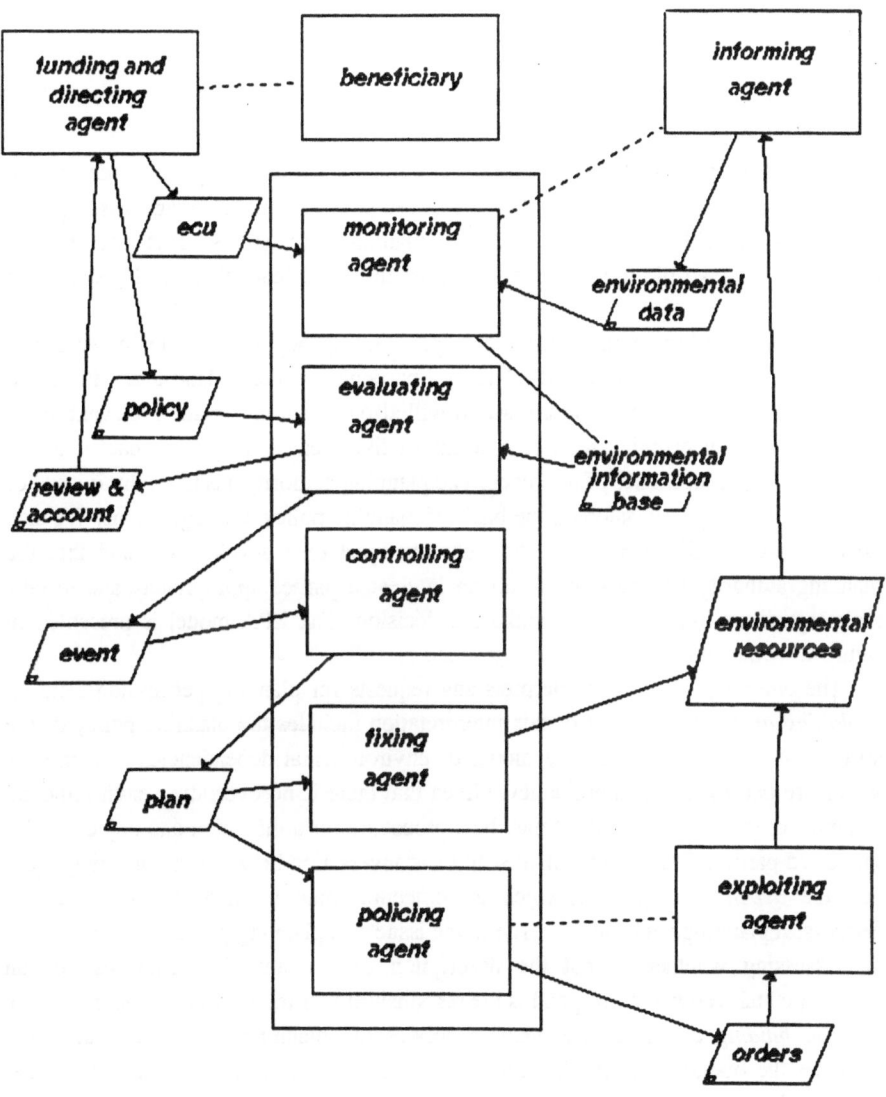

Figure 4.6 The environmental protection agency

The *controlling agent* interprets the events and trends identified by the evaluating agent in order to formulate plans to remedy their consequences. The context for this interpretation includes the environmental protection policy and the resource budget. Different aspects of such a plan will be implemented by each of the following agents:

The *repairing agent* executes remedial actions.

The *policing agent's* role is to educate, restrain and apprehend exploiters of the environment whose activities are judged to be actually or potentially damaging. Laws and regulations are the context of such judgments.

3.3 The land use planning model

The second model is relatively simple: it represents the set of agencies required to implement a land use planning policy. In developing this model, many assumptions have been made based loosely on U.K. planning procedures. This will require validation and possible modification to reflect the 1990 land planning legislation of Lombardia.

The central information resource of a planning agency is a register of land use. Each entry in such a register will relate to a particular parcel of land and will record current use and the policy for future use. It will also contain information relevant to the evaluation of any planning request in terms of likely environmental impact within a number of different frames of reference. The planning authority has the right to issue or withhold planning permission on the basis of planning policy and regulations. We also assume that outside agents have the right to object to a development and that the planning authority has the duty to inform interested parties appropriately and to take their arguments into account in making a decision. The EPA model is presented in figure 4.7 which contains the following agencies.

The *planning agent*, who interprets any requests for planning permission from an *exploiting agent*. The context of this interpretation includes the planning policy of the specific area in question and the model of environmental dependencies and impacts which are part of the planning policy. Given that there is no overriding environmental principle or policy at stake, there may be a procedure for notification and objections by interested parties. This is implemented in the conversation between the planning agent and the *depending agent* in which an objection may be lodged and evaluated. Successful planning applications result in the issue of a planning permission certificate.

Assessing whether or not the description of use and the actual use of an environmental resource correspond is the responsibility of the *inspecting agent*.

The *funding and directing agent* generates the planning policy and rules and allocates the budget that the planning agent consumes in discharging its obligations. We use this agent as a device to represent the whole policy "superstructure". It is assumed that the relationship existing between both the exploiting and depending agents and the directing agent is one of civil authority and that the instruments of this relationship are the planning acts and regulations.

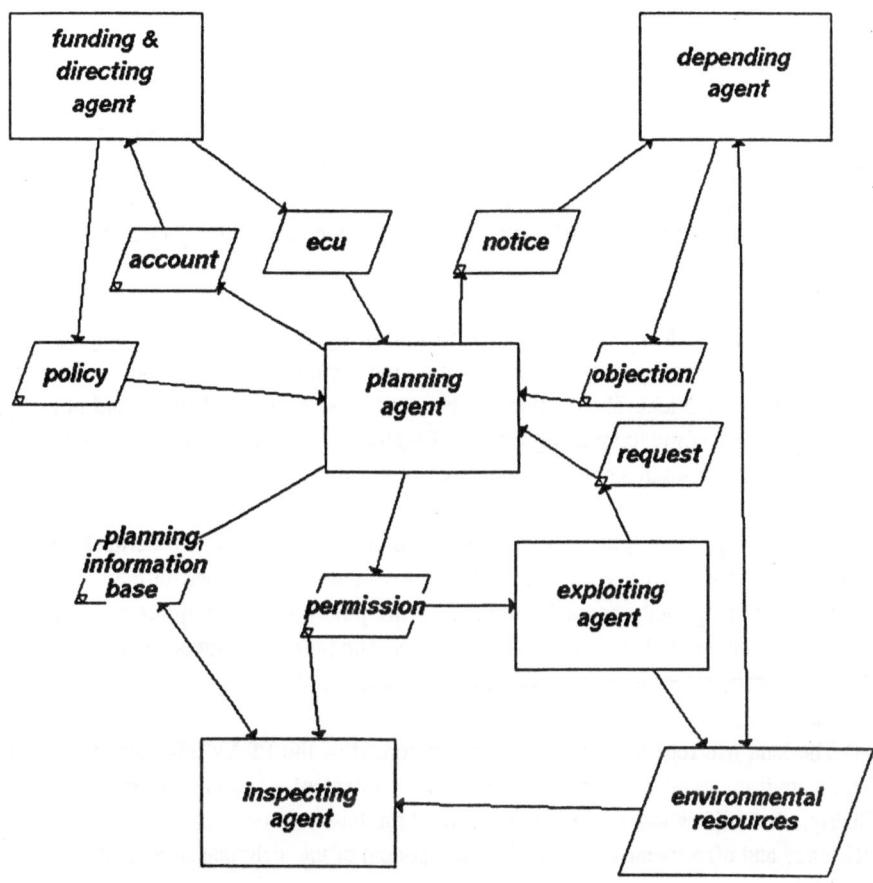

Figure 4.7 The planning agency

3.4 Participation in decision making

There are, according to the model, two distinct forms of involvement in a planning decision.

(i) Participating in planning agency and being responsible for a planning decision to the directing and resourcing agent.

(ii) Participating in the planning process as an applicant or objector.

Any application of the concept of co-operative decision making must recognise this distinction. The concept is applicable to the first category but not compatible with the relationship between first and second sorts of agency.

3.5 The relationship between the planning and protection models

The models we have presented may be concatonated. Agents that are necessarily identical are represented only once in the resulting model which we can analyse to identify common resources and dependencies. Such a model is presented in figure 4.8, and the following observations may be made on the interaction between the two original models.

(i) There is a great deal of overlap between informing agency and inspecting agency. They could, to a large extent, be discharged by the same set of actions though they are not necessarily identical. The relationship between these agents and fixing and policing agency presents some interesting issues. Together, these represent the "front line" agencies and must act in a co-ordinated way.

(ii) The issuing of a planning certificate could be an event as defined in the environment protection agency model. The EPA could be informed through a notice but the more integrated approach required by the policy makers implies a far greater degree of involvement between the two agencies. The protection agencies participate in planning agency rather than act in the role of objector on the basis of a planning notice.

(iii) The land use register is a necessary component of the EPA's information set, the EPA's environmental records are part of the context of planning decision making. Clearly, the unification of the two information bases affords great advantages of efficiency and effectiveness and is a key component of the technical support strategy.

(iv) Since the evaluation of threats, vulnerabilities and consequences in overlapping domains characterises both the enterprises, there will probably be common, underlying decision models: they are asking "what if ?" questions about the same sorts of things.

We represent the resource managing agents in this model. The EPA has a co-ordinating role in relation to these agents who are assumed to operate under a set of rules and policies which are ultimately traceable to the directing agent, i.e. the civil authority. It is the case that these rules include an operational duty to report particular environmental information to the EPA. The resource managing agents co-ordinate the operations of exploiting agents usually by issuing permits for specific instances of use. They may also operate a tariffing system whereby the exploiting agent pays for use of the resource.

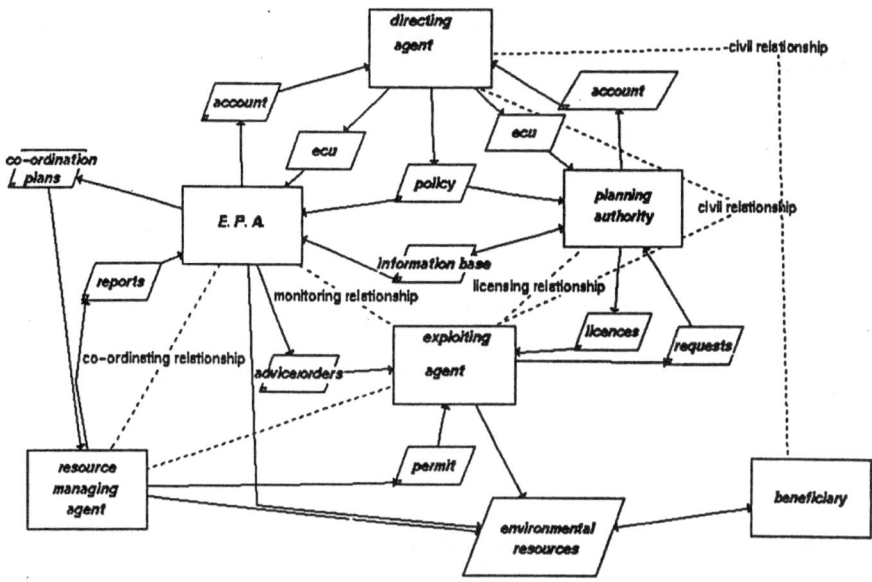

Figure 4.8 Environment protection, planning and management

A conversation which is not shown explicitly in figure 4.8 is part of the civil relationship whereby exploiting agents may request or demand a change in policy (Cf. the democratic process, the Mafia....)

In this model we see three distinct access modes to the environmental resource: use, either by right as with the beneficiary or by licence as an exploiter, control exercised by the managing agents and inspection.

3.6 Distribution policies

We have presented the models so far as if there is one, abstract protection agency, one abstract planning agency and a single overall directing and resourcing agency. In the real case study there are multiple instances of each of these agencies representing different distribution and structuring policies.

The regional EPA is structured into three sub-agencies on the basis of the different classes of environmental resource. Thus we have the Air, Water and Solid Waste agencies. Their funding and directing agent is the regional government.

There will be four distinct planning authorities each with its own funding and directing agent. These correspond to the four provinces, Milano, Como, Varese, and Pavia. Each of these contains many municipal authorities.

Several different instances of exploiting agents are identified in the case study including:

Drinking water providers

Mineral water extractors

Hydro-electric and water power

Irrigation

Industrial users, e.g. cooling, cleaning, effluent...

Navigation.

Each of these enterprises will operate under planning permission and licence and will be subject to inspection. The licensing authorities may be regarded as separate enterprises each with its own policy expressed in terms of its particular view of the environmental resource. Whether and to what extent they participate in planning decision making or protection agency is a matter of policy.

3.7 The application of the cooperation model

The first impressions as to the location and type of co-operative framework which responds to the needs and structure of this case study relate to the common ownership, maintenance and exploitation of a complex and dynamic information resource and to the need for multi-party co-operation in evaluation and decision making.

The former does not seem to appear in the other case study and requires further analysis. The model of the decision conference does, at first sight, seem applicable to the latter as is the concept of a decision support model through which the consequences of events and decisions as seen from the point of view and in terms of the specific concepts of the different stake holders may be explored.

There appears to be scope for two distinct decision conferences corresponding to the discharge of evaluation and control responsibilities within a protection agency and the exercise of planning agency.

The same question arises in the case of this model as in the previous study: Is a complete and detailed domain specific model required, in this case of the environment and of impact on it? Is such a model feasible, is one available? How does such a model relate to the enterprise issues and relationships that we have identified in our requirements modelling and how could it be deployed in the context of a co-operative decision conference?

4. Comparing the two studies

Further investigation may show that there is a common core of tools and systems which could serve co-operative aspects of both these applications domains. Such tools could be built round the following elements.

(i) A set of generic decision conferencing functions which support, for example, the role of facilitator and which promote a sound concept of the consultation and group decision making process.

(ii) A set of decision modelling functions which support the analysis of vulnerabilities and consequences in terms of commercial, legal or contractual relationships and which may be used as a medium of discussion.

(iii) A set of facilities for the generation, management and exploitation of shared, dynamic information resources.

5 Intelligent computer support

José Cuena, Ana García-Serrano

1. Introduction

The design of a computer support environment for cooperation must be based on the set of agreed organization procedures defined in a previous conceptual modelling phase (chapter 4). Two modes of computer support may be conceived:

(i) *Passive support:* in this mode, data and text communication services are provided. This is the state of the art of office automation techniques: a set of information resources is shared by several users according to an access protocol consistent with the different responsibilities of the agents. The cooperative procedures are learned and operated by the human agents belonging to the team.

(ii) *Active support:* this is an emergent innovative mode where a software system is able to represent the structure of the problem being solved by human agents, and participates by evaluating the problem state, by proposing the next tasks to be done, or by deciding whether the answers obtained from the human agents are admissible. In this case the computer provides intelligence for coordination, where additional improvements of efficiency can be obtained because, in general, the work of any organization is done as a set of cooperation procedures that satisfy some cooperation protocols. This organizational activity can be improved with an active CSCW system that allows parallel coordination. The system generates cooperation procedures consistent with protocols for situations in which several activities may be executed in parallel.

Systems for active support are beginning to appear now, as a natural development of the CSCW field. However, in the field of distributed Artificial Intelligence we can find several proposals, developed for cooperative distributed problem solving (CDPS), which may be adapted for models of CSCW where human-based and computer-based knowledge agents cooperate to meet the goals of an organization. An architecture format and methodology can be defined for designing this type of Intelligent Coordination System from a knowledge level perspective. Some attempts have been made along these lines, for instance by Nirenburg & Lesser (1986), who propose a knowledge-based approach to support cooperation in an office system, and by Croft & Lefkowitz (1988), who propose an approach to support cooperation in planning using a knowledge-based model of negotiation.

The present chapter describes first the different antecedents in the area of CSCW and CDPS, after an architecture for CSCW is proposed and an outline of a methodology for intelligent CSCW design is finally presented.

2. The active support scenario

This section presents a brief description of some existing CSCW applications that may be considered active support. There follows an overview of the CDPS state of the art from the perspective of its potential applications on CSCW. Finally, as a consequence, a classification by level of intelligent support is proposed for CSCW, deduced from the potentialities of both approaches.

2.1 Some existing CSCW applications

The existing applications presented in the area of active support of cooperative work deal mainly with the following areas.
(i) Conversational structures for email communications to produce joint documents and to classify and store structured items of a conversation.
(ii) New structures and models for structured discussions providing active support facilities such as coherence and consistency, oriented to group decision making, and support for meetings or software development.

An example is the SYBIL system (Lee 1990), which supports group decision making in areas such as the choice of an optimal hardware platform for project development, or the distribution of available floor space.

The cooperative work supported by SYBIL is the deliberation among a group of people to reach a final decision. Such computer support may be considered active. The system contains problem-solving knowledge based mainly on the MYCIN paradigm for evidence accumulation, with the difference that the evidence is linked to proposals by the members of the group. In this way a goal is proposed with several possible alternative values. The participants suggest possible subgoals of this main goal, and evidence is accumulated for these subgoals too, in such a way that the computer support system keeps track of the tree of goals and subgoals and the different claims for and against, in order to propose a final balance of the different positions.

The language for supporting this procedure is an extension of the IBIS language with sentences modelling the different viewpoints on how a subgoal should be decomposed. An example of this approach is presented in figure 5.1, where several viewpoints equivalent to different rules in MYCIN express the decomposition of a goal in subgoals. Positions about the subgoals may be based also on alternative decompositions, or may be evaluations by the different users which are propagated and accumulated to produce a final proposal for common positions about the final goal.

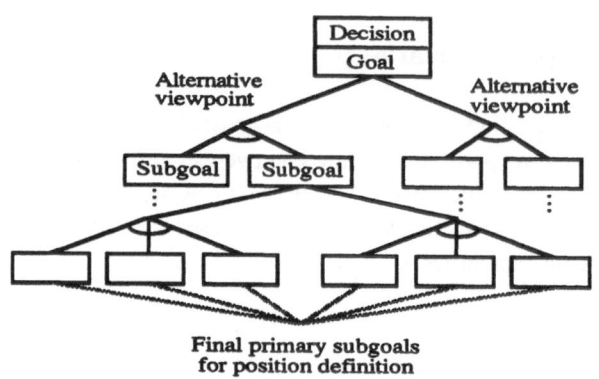

Figure 5.1 The logical structure of cooperative reasoning about a goal

As Lee (1990) points out, there may be problems in introducing such systems, either because users resist new methods or because they lack the necessary background: such problems must be balanced against the improvements that the system provides for cooperation.

Another example is the Mini-Callisto system (Sathi et al 1988), which uses the distributed problem solving paradigm in order to provide some project management support. This system was designed to deal with incomplete project knowledge, resource distribution, and changes of order in schedule revisions. It includes constraint-directed negotiation for managing resources, activities, and configurations.

The STRUDEL system (Shepherd et al 1990), which supports the cooperative development of actions (software defect tracking and repair) or the scheduling of meetings, is a further significant example.

The computer support here provides a conceptual structure for conversations through which tasks are assigned to achieve a given goal, or meetings are scheduled. The system embodies a formal model of the different messages supporting a negotiation process for task assignment among different agents. This is done by the definition of a set of labels for messages identified as names of conversational moves, in such a way that a move is associated with the set of moves that are appropriate responses.

Since the system is unable to understand the contents of the message, the only semantics is provided by the move labels. It is also reported that the users often reject the conceptual label structure and use only the communication service. The problems of labelling could be surmounted if the system could understand natural language well enough to infer labels from the message content; this would provide a more user-friendly system interface.

Despite these user problems, this project shows a first system where an abstract model of an intelligence monitors cooperative work for planning.

Information Lens (Malone et al 1988) is an intelligent system for information sharing in organizations. A set of semi-structured messages is defined so as to allow the construction of different automatic aids, such as intelligent suggestions for reply messages, local or central classification, and management messages (through rules, in the AI sense, including local ones written by the user).

The VS system (Beard et al 1990) may also be considered an active support system for planning. It is a visual scheduling facility designed to help arrange meetings, taking into account the present commitments of the people to attend a meeting. The system allows the visual presentation of personal agendas in such a way that the level of grey is an intuitive evaluation of the level of business of every day. The system uses information about priorities, based on the meeting types, in such a way that proposals for potential dates for meetings are produced, and existing meetings of lower priority can be shifted to another time. On the basis of these inferences, a new configuration of the agendas is proposed. The system is a simple example of communication and planning services.

Some of these examples show that in the present state of the art (the above systems were presented at a recent international CSCW conference) there exists an evolution towards cooperative problem solving among different human agents. Some researchers are interested in transferring concepts developed in the field of distributed Artificial Intelligence for Cooperative Distributed Problem Solving (CDPS) to CS design for CW, where more conceptually advanced models have been proposed.

2.2 CDPS approaches for supporting cooperative work

In Artificial Intelligence, problems are traditionally defined by an initial state specification I, and a goal state specification G. The problem-solving knowledge to deal with a class of problems $<I, G>$ is defined by a set of operators together with a set of rules which enable the system to choose among the applicable operators at every stage of the solution search process.

The traditional Artificial Intelligence problem-solving approaches (Nilsson 1980) are (1) state space search and (2) problem decomposition based on *means end analysis*. In the former, a tree representing states of the problem environment is seached: at each node, reasoning is performed to decide which operators are applicable and in which order they should be explored; the tree is developed until some, or all, of the solution states are found (figure 5.2). In means end analysis a reasoning step is performed to decompose the problem in subproblems in such a way that an *and/or tree* of subproblems is produced, until basic problems solvable by direct application of an operator are obtained (figure 5.3).

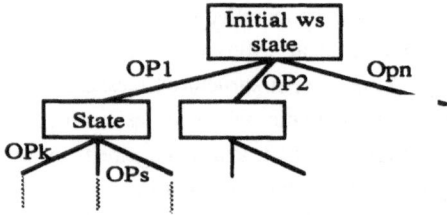

Figure 5.2 The state space search approach to problem solving

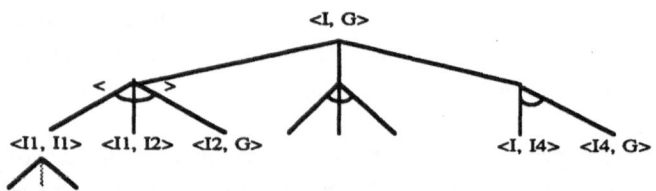

Figure 5.3 The problem decomposition approach to problem solving

The distributed problem-solving approach is based on the distribution of the knowledge and data to develop the problem solution in such a way that several agents are defined as local problem solvers. Each agents has:
(i) a partial set of operators for local problem solving;
(ii) local information;
(iii) specific local knowledge about control decisions.
The agents are integrated in a communication network which allows each agent access to a part of the information about the state of some of the other agents.

The important issues in CDPS design are (1) how to resolve interactions between the subproblems to be solved by the different agents, (2) how to control the activities among agents to exploit parallelism and (3) how to integrate partial local results into a complete global result.

The problem concept previously defined may be considered as a unit of cooperative work in such a way that CSCW software environments could be conceived as set of tools to support the cooperation of a group of human or software agents to solve one or several problem types. This would be a more general definition of the CSCW that could be supported by the addition of CDPS Artificial Intelligence concepts to the current applications of CSCW.

There are two modes for CDPS (Durfee, Lesser & Corkhill 1989):

(i) Cooperation at step level, which integrates the actions of the agents at a stage of the problem solving process.

(ii) Cooperation at plan level, where coordination among agents is formulated at the level of the future plans of the different agents.

In the first approach conflicts are detected when they are produced; in the second approach conflicts may be prevented because an agent may have information not only about present activities of another node but about its planned activities. The second approach requires more work by the local problem solvers (which produce future plans, not just the next feasible actions) and a bigger communication interchange, but the plan coordination approach is required when an unexpected conflict may produce irreversible damage.

Within the first approach, several paradigms have been proposed for cooperation:

(i) Negotiation (Smith & Davis 1981; Kornfeld & Hewitt 1981);

(ii) Functionally accurate cooperation (FA/C) (Lesser & Corkill 1981; Hewitt 1986);

(iii) Organizational structure (Corkill & Lesser 1983).

The second approach is represented by the multiagent planning field (Cammarata et al 1983; Georgeff 1983, 1984, 1986). Finally, a proposal for a flexible approach has been made by Durfee & Lesser (1987).

The first model of negotiation was proposed by Smith & Davis (1981; see also Davis & Smith 1983) with the contract net protocol, in which a distributed problem decomposition protocol is defined by the following steps:

(i) Every agent produces a step of problem decomposition deducing a set of subproblems to be solved. Some of these subproblems may be studied by the agent itself; others will lie beyond its knowledge capacity. To solve these subproblems the agent acts as a manager offering the subtasks to the other agents.

(ii) If at the next step an agent has no important task in progress, it submits a bid to the "calls for proposals" of the other agents.

(iii) The agents acting as managers receive the different proposals and award contracts to the most relevant ones; the same task could be assigned to several agents that produce different solutions.

This cycle (decompose, ask for proposals, make bids, assign tasks) is repeated until no agent has a problem to offer to the market. At this moment the execution may produce several solutions.

The knowledge of a cooperating agent acting in the framework of the contract net approach is of several types:

(i) *Knowledge for contracting*, capable of answering questions about:

   Identification of tasks to contract out;

   Abstraction of task specification, to be understood by the other agents;

Choice of agents to be informed of a contract type;

Deciding how many bidding nodes should receive the task in a set of proposals.

(ii) *Knowledge for submitting proposals*, capable of answering questions about:

Matching level of task announcement to the abstract pattern of the node's capabilities;

Evaluating the degree of difficulty of a task, to decide if the node can perform it;

Evaluating the benefits (there may be other more interesting announcements).

(iii) *Knowledge for solving several classes of subproblems,* described by rules or by operator models (preconditions for application, and add/delete lists for properties produced by applying an operator.

Much of the knowledge required to implement this cooperation model may be obtained by administering a suitable questionaire to human operators. Thus, switching from software to human agent means that knowledge bases capable of performing several tasks are substituted by intelligent interfaces which can get these tasks done by soliciting help from humans.

When the network receives a large problem, the agent nodes recursively decompose the problem until non-decomposable tasks remain, assign subproblems to nodes through contract net protocol, solve the subproblems in parallel, and synthesize one or more answers from the subproblem solutions existing in the different nodes.

Although the contract net provides an example of automated network organization, there is an evident overhead to pay for this flexibility in the contract specification, proposals bidding, and contract assignment process.

Another negotiation paradigm is the scientific community metaphor proposed by Kornfeld & Hewitt (1981). In this paradigm the agents propose new questions (goals) or answers (results) in a common file. This information may be used by the others agents of the community as a point of departure for their own work. There is a simulation of funding to control activity in the network by requiring that every goal to be analysed must have a sponsor, and every sponsor (a type of agent) must be defined with limited resources, so the resulting cooperative behaviour develops feasible and sponsored goals.

Negotiation behaviour as a basis for cooperative work among human agents may happen in the case where several persons or companies must collaborate in a flexible way to produce a common goal (or a common project) and no structural constraints are imposed (i.e. everybody may work on problems that lie within their technical and economical capabilities). As will be shown later, some constraints specifing limits on agent operation are usually required for modelling organizational structure.

The approach proposed by Lesser & Corkill (1981), called "functionally accurate cooperation", defines a style of problem solving in the presence of uncertainty. There is a set of nodes, responsible for different tasks which must be performed with overall consistency, but the individual agents have incomplete knowledge. Each node behaves as follows.

(i) It generates tentative results based on estimations of the missing premises.

(ii) It detects inconsistencies between its tentative partial results and those received from the other nodes.

(iii) It updates the tentative results using the detected inconsistencies.

This approach was used in the Distributed Vehicle Monitoring Testbed (DVMT), in which there is a set of problem solvers which receive sensor information about the vehicles moving in a particular area. Each problem solver receives partial information; through cooperation among the agents, reasonable hypotheses about vehicle trajectories are produced. All the problem solvers have the same blackboard-based architecture, together with a knowledge base that could solve the total problem if it received data from every sensor. This approach requires a lot of communication and problem solving effort. By limiting the information and communication effort for each individual problem solver, simpler problems are solved in parallel, the only additional requirement being consistency analysis in different iterations. The approach is more computer-oriented and less portable to the CSCW scenario, because it is difficult to find a set of human agents that cooperate so loosely. It is summarized in figures 5.4 and 5.5 which compare the cases of single and multiple problem-solvers.

The organizational structure of a CDPS system is a *prestablished pattern* of information and control relationships among the agents, along with a distribution of problem-solving capabilities. Some of the results produced by contracting may be obtained more efficiently by using this prestablished structure, though at the price of flexibility.

Figure 5.4 Centralized approach: all the data have to be sent to the central agent

The main design criteria for this structure are as follows.

(i) Coverage: every subproblem required for the solution must lie within the capabilities of some agent.

(ii) Connectivity: the links defined by the structure must ensure the integration of the different partial solutions into an overall solution.

(iii) Capability: the communication and computation resources available in the network must be capable of managing the problems to be solved.

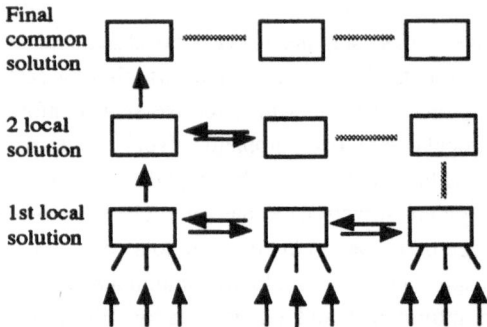

Figure 5.5 Distributed approach: data are sent to the nearest agent (a datum may be sent to several agents) and the agents communicate solution proposals

To meet these goals the structure defines:

(1) *Problem-solving roles* to be assigned to the agents so every agent may behave as a specialist in a subproblem type. This assignment of competence must be done in a redundant way to ensure that no agent is irreplaceable.

(2) *Connectivity information* in every node about the skills of the other agents. This information will be used for routing subproblems to appropriate agents.

(3) *Control authority*, which may vary from self-directed (favouring problem-solving actions based on locally generated partial results) to externally-directed (favouring actions based on partial results received from other nodes), with intermediate levels favouring negotiated actions based on internal and external results. These levels may be defined for different subsets of the actions of an agent. Every agent may operate either in data-driven mode, or in goal-directed mode, or through task assignment.

Corkill and Lesser have experimented with these ideas in the DVMT just described, establishing a structure among nodes and proposing a blackboard architecture for the agents with the organization structure defined in the KSs of the agents. The idea of architectures within an organization structure permits the experiment of translating existing developments in the field of social organizations to societies of computing agents. Further experiments are needed to evaluate the efficiency of these social concepts in the more structured world of computerized agents.

This CDPS paradigm is clearly portable to the CSCW scenario because the capabilities for different subproblems may be defined by sets of operators for problem-solving which model both agent abilities and organizational structure. Moreover, constraints may be defined which model the organization structure criteria for task assignment to agents.

In the approach of multiagent planning, the nodes (agents) form a multiagent plan that specifies all their future actions and interactions. Coordination at this plan level requires that nodes share and process substantial amounts of information, develop more complex computations, and communicate more than they do in other approaches.

However, multiagent planning avoids inconsistent or conflicting actions in the near future. It is very convenient for air traffic scheduling or machining tools, since in these tasks a conflict may produce irreversible problems. Corkill (1979) proposed an initial model of distributed multiagent planning based on the criterion that each node should build a local plan at one level of detail and build suitable models of each other by communicating about shared resources needed for their goals. Once a level is balanced, the agents proceed to the next level until a detailed plan is produced. Rosenschein & Genesereth (1987) studied how agents with a common goal but different local information can exchange propositions to converge on identical plans. They proved that convergence on a plan cannot be guaranteed.

In the CSCW field this state of affairs is found when a set of agents must collaborate to build an integrated product using results from different suppliers: examples are public works planning, building planning, and satellite planning, all of which require the integration of several technologies in a common product.

2.3 Active CSCW: a proposed classification

Knowledge structuring may be approached from the knowledge level perspective. According to Newell (1982), intelligent systems should be designed by an initial phase of identifying the goals and knowledge that would be required by an ideal agent, capable of solving problems in a given environment by applying its knowledge according to the principle of rationality.

Considering an organization from an external viewpoint as this ideal agent, its operational capabilities for solving problems in a given environment could be described by the following:
- the set of common goals of the organization;
- the set of operational agents that are components of the organization (human and data based), each applying different agencies to solve different problems;
- the set of cooperation (rational) protocols allowing the creation of different cooperation procedures to meet the organization's goals.

Systems analysis techniques might provide an adequate description of an organization at this level.

To develop computer support for this knowledge level description of an organization, a symbolic representation of these concepts must be defined. Two types of knowledge need to be represented:
- Knowledge for modelling the internal agreements for cooperation, together with common knowledge about the problems to be solved cooperatively;
- Knowledge for modelling the capabilities of the individual operational agents.

This may also be analysed at the knowledge level by describing the various goals

and the knowledge associated with them, assuming that part of this knowledge
may be provided by humans.

Different levels of intelligence may be conceived for the computer support of
coordination, according to the functions to be supported in the cooperation model and
the agent model:

(A) Data communication service: This corresponds to the common database facility
mentioned above. Data and text are available in a central computer, or distributed in
several computers through a network where different data and texts may be stored and
used by the various cooperating agents.

(B) Data communication and evaluation service: Under this category the computer
system must provide:

- Syntactic evaluation of the different predefined message structures (similar to the
  previous level.
- Semantic evaluation: the message content is interpreted, and this interpretation
  is checked for consistency with the mission of every agent and the current state
  of the work in progress, so that an initial level of conceptual filtering is provided
  by the system and sent to the different cooperating agents. The answers of the
  system may be used by the agents as the starting point of a discussion.

The computer system contains knowledge bases for understanding different problem
patterns. The operation of the agent generates a set of messages about the current
cooperative work task corresponding to a predefined model of cooperative problem
solving. The system receives the new messages and is able to obtain data about the
problem state and to reason about the progress of the problem on the basis of the
message content. The system reaches conclusions about the level of progress; for
instance, it may understand that a solution has been found or that a contradictory
situation has been presented.

(C) Diagnostic service: This service may be integrated with the previous one because
when a solution or a dead end for backtracking is identified, an explanation based on
the knowledge of the system could be provided in cases for which some possible
causes are given for the contradictory situations.

(D) Predictive capacity: In some cases it may be important that the system provides
information not only about what happens but also about what might happen. An
example is the case of evaluation when, in the current situation, several causes for
future problems can be identified. The system must be able to predict these future
problems by using some kind of behaviour model. This occurs for instance when
contamination has been detected in areas where waste has been deposited, with the
consequence that city water problems may be predicted.

In such cases of predictive capacity the operation of the system requires two steps
of analysis:

- Evaluation and explanation of the present situation;
- Short term scenario prediction and evaluation of potential future problems;
followed by a final explanation step.

(E) Planning capability: When a set of disfunctions has been identified, the system proposes possible actions or intermediate goals to meet the final goals. For instance, if the system finds that the current course of the project has not met some intermediate objectives, and with predictive reasoning it can be inferred that some other goals may be missed, proposals for reorganizing the task may be put forward. In offering this service the system does not suggest which agents should perform the various tasks: it just suggests new cooperative goals, or new tasks to be performed by the group.

In this category may be included the cooperative decision-making systems which derive consensus solutions on the basis of the solutions suggested by the participants.

(F) Distributed planning capability: When a set of tasks has been identified, the system monitors a task assignment procedure. This may be done by using either the negotiation paradigm or the organizational paradigm, as mentioned above. When the proposed tasks are analyzed by the cooperating agents, some proposals for its partial or total development may be submitted by the different agents. After identifying which residual subtasks have not yet been assigned, the system may propose a second round of task assignment ... and so on. If the organizational structure paradigm is used, the system may embody knowledge about task or subtask assignment in a form consistent with the responsibilities of the different agents defined by the organization.
This is the most sophisticated service to be proposed for a CSCW system that collaborates with people.

(G) Distributed planning capability and agent knowledge modelling: This is the maximum level of computer support, in which humans are replaced by knowledge-based models of the agent capabilities. This is the level of CDPS, where there is a single application from the user point of view but the cooperation structure is internal to the application, so that the system supports both the cooperation management and the work itself.

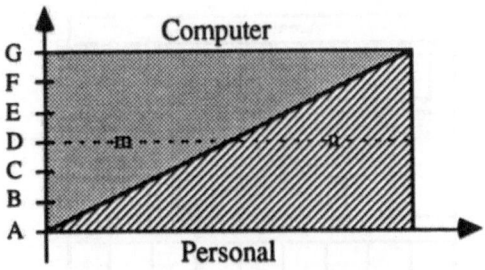

Figure 5.6 The different levels of computer support
(m = computer supported activity; n = human supported activity)

These different categories of computer support are summarized in figure 5.6; the diagonal shows the frontier between human and computer support.

3. An architecture for intelligent CSCW

Before designing computer support, the user organization should be modelled in order to identify a set of agents, which can be either organizations or individuals integrated into the general organization, and a set of cooperation protocols through which the operational aims of the organization can be realized. These protocols represent the way in which the different agent missions interact.

At this preliminary stage, cooperative problem solving may be understood as human or organizational problem solving - that is, as an integration of tasks which may be performed by people in the organization and which achieve the desired objective.

The following sections define the types of knowledge unit and propose a knowledge architecture.

3.1 Types of knowledge unit

We define two types of knowledge unit. The first is the *general facilitation task*, which embodies the knowledge for intelligent control and monitoring of a predefined cooperation protocol. It has the following components (figure 5.7):
- A set of message inputs from the agents in a predefined structure;
- A problem state area that specifies the goals to be pursued;
- A set of messages to be sent to the agents;
- A knowledge base modelling the cooperation protocols and general knowledge needed for the current operation;
- An inference procedure modelling the cooperation strategy appropriate for the current task.

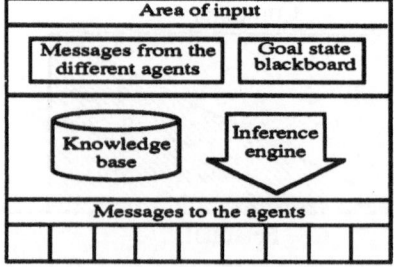

Figure 5.7 The general facilitation task

The tasks here identified provide the basis for an environment for designing cooperation models, so that intelligent support systems for the required level of coordination can be developed step by step. For the different types of task, several kinds of knowledge content can be considered.

(i) Basic facilitation tasks such as:

- Dialogue supervision by controlling the syntactic structure of messages, with sufficient semantic understanding to judge their adequacy (the issue/position/ argument structure of the IBIS method).
- State space search problem solving when agents suggest different ways of developing the current problem state.
- Problem decomposition when using means-end analysis; for example, through simulated negotiation an initial problem is divided into several subproblems until a set of solvable problems is found.
- Cooperative decision making when different perspectives propose contradictory evaluations of a decision and a process to consensus must be monitorized.
- Cooperative plan repair.

(ii) A compound facilitation task designed to help in the performance of complex cooperation procedures where the use of several basic facilitator tasks may be integrated in its knowledge base. Several levels of complexity may be conceived where a main facilitator acts as the general manager of other compound or basic facilitation tasks.

A second type of knowledge unit is the *agent environment*, which embodies the knowledge needed for communication with the system and with human users.

Durfee (1988) proposes a standard for agent knowledge representation, based on a blackboard structure that includes KS for internal problem-solving knowledge and for external agents proposals for subproblems to solve. This type of structure, or something similar, should be the final aim, but for integrating human agents we propose a simpler arrangement with two blackboards:

(1) A problem state blackboard that contains relevant contributions of local and external agents for the current problem. Messages on this blackboard should conform to a standard structure (e.g. the IBIS format of issue/position/argument in natural language for human comprehension, and an internal knowledge language for computerized agents and facilitators).

(2) A subproblem state blackboard that contains intermediate goals organized into an agenda of current tasks to be performed either by the local agent or by external agents.

A conventional interface system will be responsible for passing messages between the coordination system and other agents. If a human agent is in charge of the problem-solving capability he will read information from these two blackboards and produce messages for the system through these interfaces.

Inside each agent environment, some intermediate situations might conceivably be presented, in which some knowledge elements are represented by knowledge bases to be controlled by the user. In fact even the user criteria might be modelled by a knowledge base. The general structure of the agent task is shown by figure 5.8.

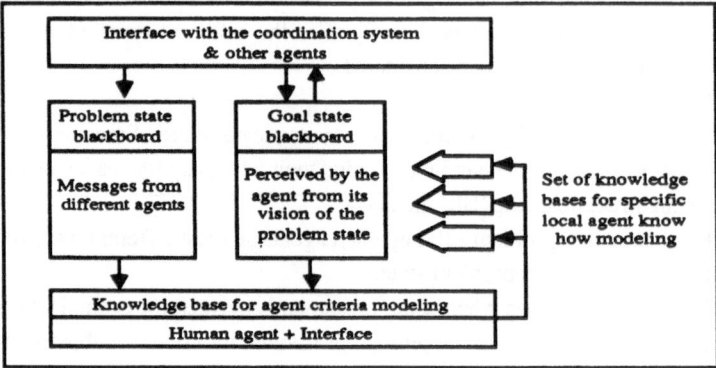

Figure 5.8 The agent task general structure

3.2 General knowledge architecture

A general knowledge architecture should be considered for designing this type of computer support.

The concept of architecture in Artificial Intelligence was introduced by Newell (1982) who distinguished the "knowledge level" at which only pieces of knowledge of predefined structure are given by the user for an application definition. An architecture is a set of conventions about knowledge representation, inference, knowledge acquisition, and learning, supported by an integrated software environment which enables users to describe problems at the knowledge level. That means that an architecture supports problem solving using knowledge-level specifications in the same way that traditional languages support the specification of procedures and data types.

Newell's ideas led to the development of the SOAR architecture (Laird et al 1987), which is based on a set of problem spaces for which different knowledge bases are defined to deal with subproblem classes. To solve a problem, the system applies a universal subgoaling procedure which activates the relevant problem spaces, starting with the most abstract. The system is a structured version of the GPS concept (Newell & Simon 1963) for solving problems by decomposition, which provides users with a structured definition of the knowledge required to deal with a class of problems. SOAR also provides a procedure for learning by chunking, which allows knowledge to be synthesized at a level resulting from a subgoaling procedure using deeper level problem spaces, so that subsequently subgoaling may be decreased by using the learned knowledge. According to the SOAR concept a user should only define the problem spaces needed to solve a class of problems. In each problem space the necessary concepts and production rules are defined to deal with the type of problem to be solved.

The SOAR experience showed, with improved performance, the advantages of developing software environments to support specialized knowledge applications.

Other experiments in this line were ICARUS (Langley et al 1990), which deals with inference in probabilistic hierarchies, and PRODIGY (Minton et al 1988), a revised and more structured version of the classical STRIPS system (Fikes, Hart & Nilsson 1971). These projects were oriented to the definition of general knowledge architectures which, although domain independent, were limited to a set of functionalities in knowledge representation, inference, knowledge acquisition, and learning.

In parallel with these developments Chandrasekaran (1983, 1986) proposed that knowledge representation models should be based on problem-solving models that were more specific than the traditional rule-based formulations. Chandrasekaran proposed the concept of "generic task" as a basis for knowledge structuring. Several software environments were developed, with task structures suitable for classes of problems such as diagnosis, by search in a hierarchy of tasks, or routine design (Brown & Chandrasekaran 1989), by search in a hierarchy of plan-level representations based on instances of generic tasks.

Alonso et al (1990) and Cuena et al (1991) proposed a complementary view to the general architecture approach in the sense that some domain-specific features could be introduced into an architecture to support *professional intelligences,* which embody a set of knowledge elements in a professional field, so that to build a knowledge model for a problem only some specific parameters must be introduced to instantiate these built-in models, together with a specific problem-solving module to control the general reasoning. This concept has been applied to build intelligent systems which predict watershed system behaviour to support decisions about flood damage. The same concept is currently being used in a project for real time traffic control advice (Cuena 1991).

According to these references, the design of knowledge-based facilitation modules could be supported by a toolset of generic tasks in the sense of Chandrasekaran (1986), Alonso et al (1990), and Cuena et al (1991). The toolset will be designed in accordance with the general structure shown in figure 5.9, which includes the following elements:
 - A facilitation general task structure;
 - A basic facilitation task structure which adds to the general structure the knowledge elements needed for a set of typical cooperation tasks;
 - An agent behaviour definition task;
 - A library of basic communication functions to be supported by a communication framework;
 - A set of basic procedures for knowledge acquisition, inference and explanation, in which for example the inference procedure must be able to interpret the main facilitator protocol so as to explore the cooperation procedures consistent with the compound facilitator model of its cooperation protocols.
Using these elements, a cooperation support problem may be modelled by:
 - A set of compound facilitators which, by using the general facilitator task structure, incorporate the specific knowledge-based models of several ad hoc organization cooperation protocols;

- A set of instances of the basic facilitator tasks to be used by the cooperation protocols;
- A set of instances of the agent tasks where different levels of intelligence may be modelled according to the degree of human participation.

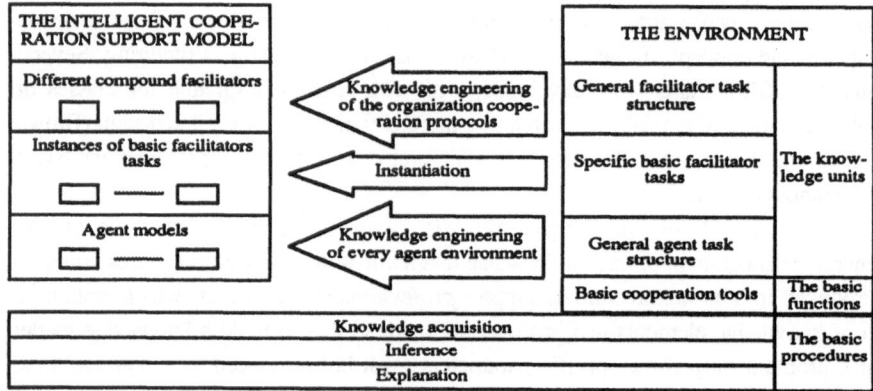

Figure 5.9 Relationships between cooperation support and environment

The general structure of a toolset for defining cooperation models will include the basic facilitator cognitive modules together with general tools for building compound facilitators of several predefined classes, so that a model for a specific cooperation procedure may be defined by knowledge elicitation of the compound facilitator and by the instanciation of basic facilitators.

The knowledge base in this case represents not the expertise in a domain, but the criteria and norms agreed by the cooperative agents; thus when discrepancies arise, changes in the cooperation knowledge can be introduced easily. The basic facilitators embody knowledge for elementary cooperation tasks such as dialogue validation, state space search problem solving, and negotiation. The compound facilitators are domain-specific procedures or search trees which model complex cooperation procedures.

The knowledge-based structure is appropriate for designing a facilitator-based architecture because a facilitator embodies the rules of every game to be played in the cooperative procedures to be performed by the organization. It is difficult to state these rules as algorithms since they will vary from one case to another according to circumstances. Thus in most cases the facilitator should be realized by a knowledge base, although a some simple cases a procedural facilitator could be designed.

Since a compound facilitator requires the integration of several basic facilitators, a modular architecture for the knowledge base is to be preferred, each module being defined as an instance of the different basic facilitator types, and controlled by a procedural or knowledge-based model of the general facilitation strategy required by the total cooperation procedure.

The knowledge based architecture is also interesting because it allows the progressive introduction in the computer support software system of different layers of facilitation in accordance with the levels of acceptance and capacity of the users. Thus it is possible to work initially with a passive support level and then, after acquiring some practical experience with the system, to add modules that support further aspects of the work which the human users may be glad to relinquish.

4. CSCW design methodology

A knowledge representation approach must be evaluated by two criteria: (1) its ability to represent the concepts and inference procedures for the type of problem to be solved; (2) the feasibility and reliability of knowledge acquisition for the structures predefined in the architecture.

The architecture proposed here satisfies both criteria by providing a guide for decomposing the problem in such as way that, at every step, manageable problems are being solved in knowledge acquisition, inference, and explanation.

On the basis of the above concepts, a methodology for intelligent computer support can be defined. It has the following main steps.

4.1 Conceptual framework definition

Before designing computer support, the user organization should be modelled in order to identify:

(i) *A set of agents.* An agent can be either an organization, or an individual integrated into the general organization. An agent may be considered as a set of local "agencies" (duties) which can contribute in various ways to the overall task. An example of such an agency would be the analysis of the current state of the project. For each agent, the definition of its agencies must be complemented by a set of internal local procedures, called "missions", with which it discharges its agencies. (Thus an agent's "agency" is the job it must do, as viewed from the outside; its "mission" is the detailed means by which the job is accomplished.) This definition it is not necessarily deterministic. The set of missions may be considered an extensional definition of the agent concept prior to the design of computer support.

(ii) *A set of cooperation protocols* through which the operational aims of the organization can be realized. These procedures represent the way in which the different agent missions interact. A cooperation protocol matches a set of organizational obligations: an organizational procedure is the result of instantiating a cooperation protocol. The agents are the actors in the performance of every cooperation procedure. Different agencies of each agent are taken into account in each step of the cooperation procedure.

When defining the cooperation procedures no reference to computer support is required: it suffices to define protocols by which the agents can achieve the proposed objectives, specifying which information and which time priorities must be respected by the human agents. In other words, the set of cooperation procedures must be agreed by the people responsible for carrying out the work, as a good framework for cooperation.

At this preliminary stage, cooperative problem solving may be understood as human or organizational problem solving - that is, as an integration of tasks which may be performed by people in the organization and which achieve the desired objective. Every organizational procedure may be described by a sequence of data operations, local and cooperative problem solving steps, and cooperative decision-making tasks. The agencies are problem-solving or evaluation tasks performed by humans.

Once the model of cooperation is specified in terms of cooperation procedures, the design of intelligent computer support can begin. Computer coordination will be based on the facilitator

This step must define the conceptual items required in any cooperation procedure with human agents.

4.2 Cooperation procedure modelling

The goal of this step is the symbolic representation of the knowledge level concepts using the elements of the proposed architecture.

(i) **Agent representation**: For each agent, a model based on the agent's task structure will be specified, with the following components:
- Data support environment, i.e. functions for receiving and sending data and structured messages from the integrated system;
- Set of final and intermediate goals that the agent may undertake by using its agencies;
- Knowledge-based support at the agent level formed by the different knowledge sources to support some of the local agencies.

(ii) **Coordination model design**: This could be accomplished by the following two steps.

(a) *Specification of the functional human-computer cooperation procedure.* This is a very important aspect because user acceptability is a key issue in cooperative support. Successive versions of the cooperation procedure must be simulated until a full agreement between user and system is obtained.

The definition of the human-computer cooperation procedure is an original feature in CSCW methodology because mixed procedures must be created which distribute tasks between people and computer facilitators. An acceptable design should satisfy the following criteria:

- Tasks assigned to humans should lie within their knowledge and capacity.
- Tasks assigned to the computer should provide intermediate results and advice that are acceptable to the human user not only because they are technically efficient but also because they respect the person's rights.
- The computer support should improve the operation procedure, as measured by such aspects as quality, time, cost, human satisfaction.

Several acceptable designs must be developed and evaluated before the final selection. During this phase. a report should be written, and a mock up of the interface should be implemented, to show the characteristics of the human-computer protocol applied to the different cooperation procedures. The human-computer cooperation procedures must not be deterministic procedures, but rather a set of rules or constraints which permit various possible operation procedures.

(b) Specification of the computer system model, using the facilities provided by the architecture described above: Using the software environment shown by figure 5.7, a series of models should be defined and evaluated until a version is found which suffices for sample case analysis. The result up to this step should be similar to the analysis model and first design model proposed in the KADS methodology (Hayward, Wielinga & Breuker 1987) for expert system design.

(iii) Sample case analysis: Once a facilitator has been formulated to support a cooperation procedure, some real world sample cases should be tried out and discussed so as to obtain deeper and more efficient knowledge to deal with the tested cases. Specific knowledge- engineering methods should be applied because in this case the knowledge is not elicited from a human expert but formulated collectively by the cooperating human agents.

This step may be organized as a cycle of *knowledge introduction - sample case simulation - knowledge revision,* until an acceptable version is reached.

Finally, when a set of cooperation procedure models for real world problems has been agreed, these models should be installed experimentally, with regular follow-up meetings to discuss any necessary modifications.

5. Models of case studies

For illustrative purposes the examples provided by Amadio and Fassina (chapter 3) are simplified in some respects.

5.1 The factory location license

This example deals with the design of the cooperation procedure for a factory location license by a set of agents in Public Administration. Two steps of the methodology are considered: first, we define a human-computer cooperation procedure; second, we propose appropriate software support.

5.1.1 Human-computer cooperation procedures

It is assumed that the organization includes a policing agent, an environmental protection agent, and a land use agent, which should evaluate a proposal for a new factory location. A possible human-computer cooperation procedure associated with this organizational procedure could be as follows.

(i) First, the policing agent receives and accepts the project for a new factory location and initiates the facilitation procedure. The main facilitator gives the decision-making facilitator authority to make a decision about the environment impact. We will assume that the environmental protection agent is organized into three cooperating subagents: the solid waste agent, the air pollution agent, and the land damage agent.

Each subagent may send messages in issue/position/argument format about the degree of agreement on several issues of the project definition. After accumulating evidence, the internal facilitator prepares a final report about the environment impact and gives it to the main facilitator.

(ii) The main facilitator asks the land use agent to produce a report about the adequacy of the new factory location.

(iii) After consulting these two reports, the main facilitator makes a final decision about the new factory licensei collaboration with the land use agent, the environmental protection agent and the policing agent, who exchange messages in issue/position/argument format iteratively until consensus is reached.

The procedure is summarized by figure 5.10.

5.1.2 Design of computer support

The basic facilitators supporting this model of cooperation are as follows.
(i) A cooperative decision-making facilitator suitable for environmental impact evaluation by the three subagents.
(ii) An issue/position/argument analysis facilitator suitable for validating messages that express opinions and justifications on environment impact. This facilitator produces an adequate input for the decision making facilitator.

(iii) An issue/position/argument analysis facilitator for validating and understanding messages from the agents dealing with license allocation (the land use and environmental protection agents).

(iv) A cooperative decision-making facilitator which plays the role of main facilitator for decision making by the environment agent, the land use agent and the policing agent.

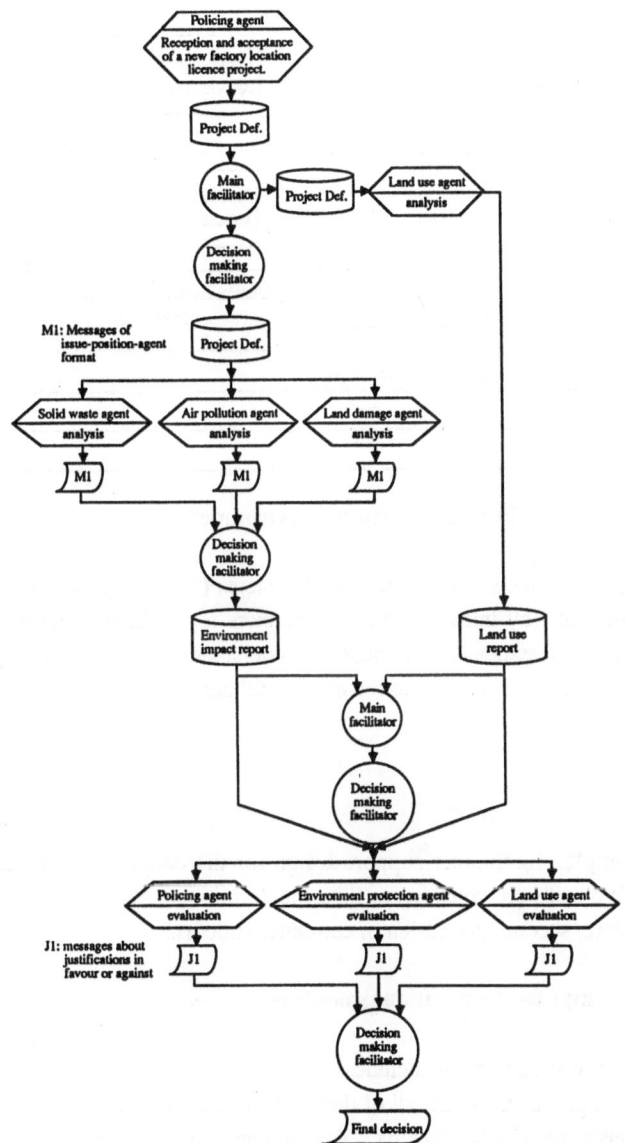

Figure 5.10 Human-computer cooperation procedure for factory location license decision

An environment could be developed to deal with understanding administrative acts and making cooperative decisions. Two generic tasks would have to be defined: one for structured message validation and understanding; the other for cooperative decision making.

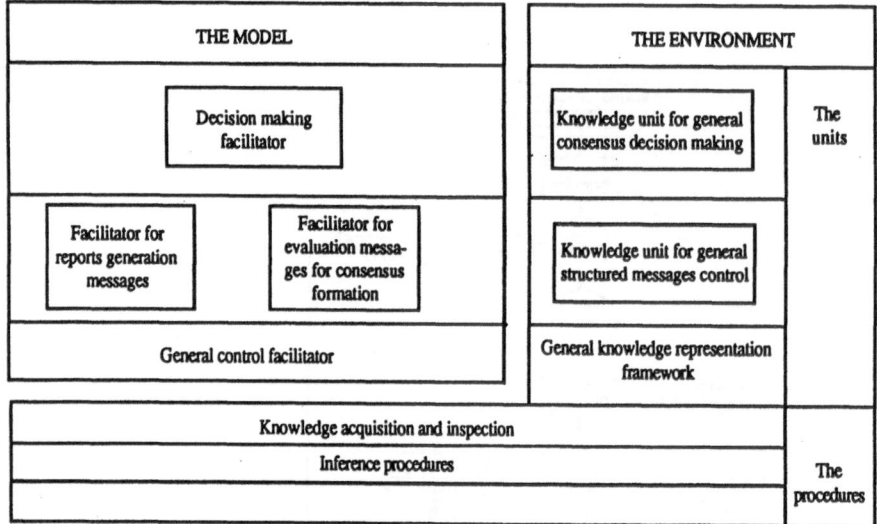

Figure 5.11 Proposed software environment

A model for such problems may be built in two steps: (1) specify two cooperative decision-making modules (by introducing the parameters for input and output and the knowledge bases); (2) instanciate the message-understanding tasks and a general control procedure which monitors calls to the main facilitator and other related tasks.

5.2 Plan generation

We present an example of computer support design for the cooperation procedure of plan generation. Two steps are considered: first, the definition of the human-computer cooperation procedure; second, the design of computer support.

5.2.1 The human-computer cooperation procedure

It is assumed that the organization includes a coordination agent, a general system designer, and several producer agents; all of these agents must collaborate to produce a work plan that meets a predefined objective - the generation of the first plan.

The cooperation procedure to be supported, in accordance with the previous description, may be conceived as a sequence of two basic procedure applications:

    - Generation of a set of feasible plans;

- Selection by cooperative decision making of the best acceptable plan.
Two main cooperation activities may be conceived to meet these goals:
  - An activity which supports plan generation by problem decomposition
    through negotiation;
  - An activity which supports the decision-making process by accumulating
    evidence from the agents confirming/disconfirming the proposed alternatives.
The cooperation procedure for the first activity is as follows.

(i) The project manager proposes several possible problem decompositions by conjunction of different macrotasks (project guidelines), with reference to the problem definition.

The problem to be solved is defined by the couple $<I, F>$, where I denotes the set of premises defining the initial state and F denotes the set of conditions defining the final state. For example, I might be the set of conditions modelling the stock of basic resources (money, time, materials, etc.), while F might be the final set of conditions modelling the products that define the project.

(ii) The various design-test agents propose several possible project decompositions for the macrotasks, with reference to the project guidelines and their own work plans. Each of these agents may define a set of possible decompositions:

$$<I, F_1> \quad <F_1, F_2> \quad ... \quad <F_k, F>$$
$$<I, G_1> \quad <G_1, G_2> \quad ... \quad <G_p, F>$$
$$... \quad ... \quad ... \quad ...$$
$$... \quad ... \quad ... \quad ...$$
$$<I, S_1> \quad <S_1, S_2> \quad ... \quad <S_q, F>$$

(iii) Next, these decompositions are analysed logically by the project manager to detect gaps or temporal inconsistencies. In this way, consistent decompositions are distinguished from inconsistent ones.

(iv) The producer agents submit proposals for partial or total execution of some subtasks among those proposed by the coordination agent. A proposal has the following parts.

(a) A chronology of tasks, each task being defined by:
   P - the set of preconditions or preceding tasks
   PS - the set of postconditions
   Time delay
   Price
   A text explaining the contents of the task
The alternative definition of the preconditions by a list of precedent tasks
is an indirect definition, which in this case may be obtained by conjoining
the valid remaining postconditions from the preceding tasks.
(b) To coordinate this activity, the submission negotiation facilitator identifies
the degree of satisfaction of every alternative decomposition, reacting in
one of the following ways:

- Call for proposals of complementary tasks to fill the gaps created by
the submissions of partial tasks (e.g. a producer agent might submit a
plan for the major subtask $<G_i, G_{i+1}>$ that solves the problem $<G_i, P>$,
in which case a complementary proposal would be needed for $<P, G_i>$.

- Ask for agreement from the producers for changes in price and time
delay: e.g. the total available budget might be less than the total budget
originally submitted, in which case the facilitator could apply rules to
propose changes in the costs and delays.

- Decide to cancel an alternative decomposition when not enough plans
are submitted for the component subtasks, or when the plans submitted
exceed by a large margin the available resources of cost and time.

-Decide to accept a plan when a set of proposals meets the specifications
to the required degree.

The latter two decisions may be generated through proposals to the coordination
agent by previous facilitator computations, or by decisions of the coordination
agent after receiving messages from the facilitator summarizing the state of the
proposals.

(c) The producer agents submit proposals for the complementary tasks.

(d) The facilitator reacts in the same way.

This process is repeated until the facilitator proposes a set of possible plans for final
analysis and no complementary submissions are required.

Final proposals from this facilitator will often fail to match all the logical, temporal,
and financial specifications; if so, a compromise decision must be made. This objective
of analysis is met by the cooperative decision making facilitator, which monitors a
process of the following kind:

(a) The main facilitator sends an initial message to the agents; this message
includes the final report on the first step and presents for each alternative a
Gantt diagram together with the logical, economic, and temporal discrepancies.

(b) Each agent answers with evaluation messages of the following form:

- Premise reasons: set of attribute values characterizing a given alternative.

- Conclusion: qualitative value of the degree of recommendation (positive
or negative).

(This is a specific version for a prefixed type of problem solving of the issue/
position/argument structure.)

(c) The facilitator uses a knowledge base to combine the different evaluations
and proposes an initial conclusion order: for instance, the first three alternatives
after the evaluation process.

(d) The agents may answer with complementary messages, and the facilitator
may repeat the analysis until equilibrium is reached.

The procedure is summarized by figure 5.12. Note that the name of the procedure
should be understood in a general sense, since a non-deterministic procedure can be

defined on the basis of a set of constraints (modelling the rules of the game) which may be satisfied by different procedures.

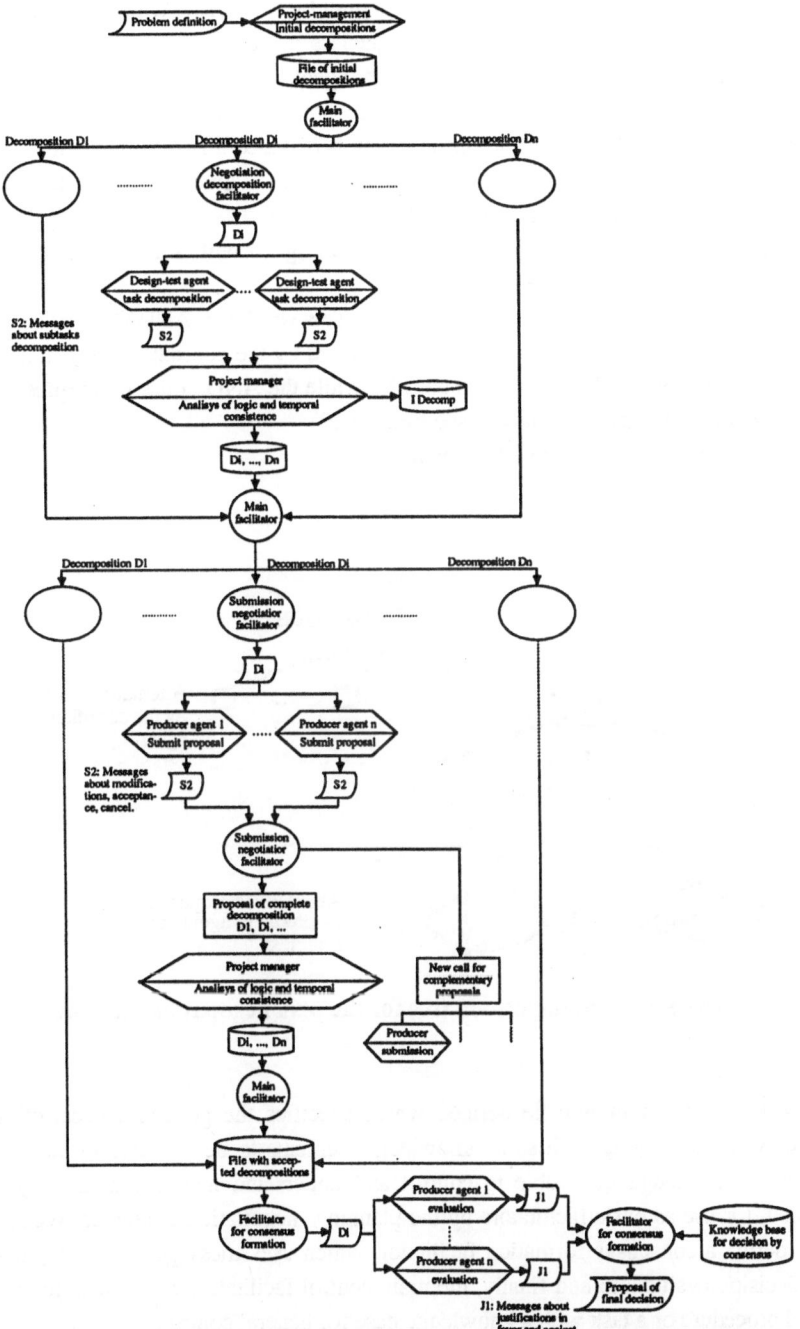

Figure 5.12 Human-computer cooperation procedure for plan design

5.2.2 The computer support

If the previously defined human-computer operation procedures are accepted, the support for cooperative plan definition will be built by two basic facilitators and a main facilitator. The main facilitator can be designed as a procedure that (1) asks for the initialization message from the coordination agent, (2) gives control to the first facilitator, and (3) sends as a final message some feasible plans to initiate the cooperative decision making. If no feasible plan is obtained a new initialization will be requested from the coordination agent; otherwise step (4) gives control to the second facilitator, which must analyze every feasible plan found.

The main plan generation facilitator may be designed with a knowledge base that reasons from the following premises:

(a) The state of the problem decomposition tree. This will be an AND/OR tree in which the OR nodes are the different alternatives proposed by the coordination agent and the alternative proposals submitted for a subtasks, while the AND nodes will represent the decomposition of a task in subtasks (see figure 5.13).

(b) The proposals submitted by each agent.

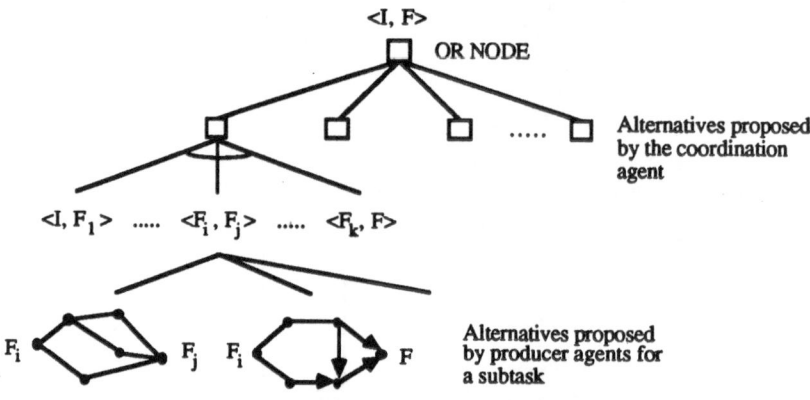

Figure 5.13 The task decomposition tree for the plan negotiation example

A knowledge unit will be defined which specifies the general aspects of these knowledge bases along with some knowledge elements to be assumed by default. In addition, knowledge units able to control and understand negotiation messages are needed, for use as basic facilitators by the planning negotiation facilitator. We should also define a consensus formation facilitator, which uses message control facilitators for decision evaluation; and finally, the main control facilitator, which will be either a fixed procedure or a task with a knowledge base for general control.

A possible environment for coordinating the development of intelligent plans is described in figure 5.14, which specifies a general message control task with three instances for the different message types to be controlled. These message control tasks must allow the composition of both structured and text versions of the messages, so that the messages are understood and validated according to their functionality. For message structuring purposes a lexicon must be compiled together with a grammar and a knowledge base for understanding; the general knowledge unit may include some common features and procedures for text production. To instantiate the unit for every mission the lexicon and grammar should be introduced together with the knowledge base for interpretation. The procedure for grammar and knowledge structure interpretation may be a general one included at the task level.

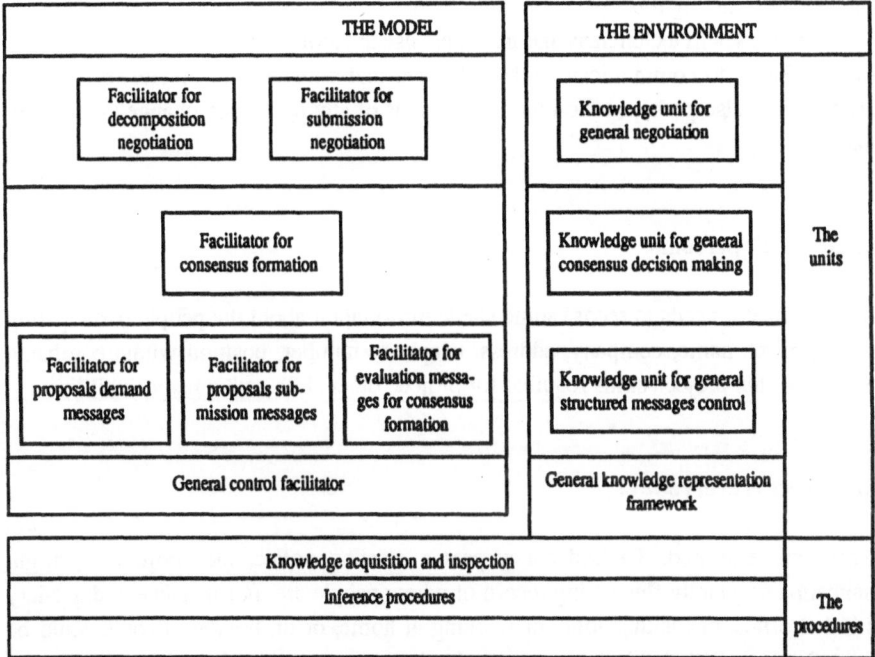

Figure 5.14 A possible software environment structure and model for plan derivation

This environment could be improved by adding further facilities for plan management: while an acceptable plan is being developed, unexpected incidents may occur, requiring the following interventions:
   (a) Understanding messages reporting incidents;
   (b) Predictive reasoning to find out which aspects of the existing plan are affected by the incident;
   (c) Renegotiation if it turns out that the plan needs to be partially modified.

6. Examples of CSCW tools

This section lists some possible tools for CSCW, especially for large projects involving several organisations. We make no attempt to formulate these tools in detail or to evaluate their usefulness.

Question: Who will use the tools?

Answer: In the first place, the coordinator. In the second place, the technicians and managers who are coordinated.

Question: In general terms, how will the coordinator use the tools?

Answer: They should allow him/her to maintain a database about the relevant tasks and people, to draw inferences from this data, and to send information, conclusions, or suggestions to the right people at the right time.

Question: How will technicians and managers use the tools?

Answer: Partly to communicate with each other and with the coordinator; partly as a news service; also perhaps to test the implications of any postulated change to the work plan.

6.1 Dramatis personae

The coordinator needs to record some stable information about the people participating in the project: name, company, address, telephone number, position within company, position within project, skills required for project, other skills, other responsibilities.

6.2 Where is everybody?

People move around. To find a key person at short notice, the coordinator might maintain a constantly fluctuating record of where people are. For instance: today Mary is in her office, or visiting John, or working at home, or on holiday. People could be obliged to report their plans on request (perhaps every week), but allowed to report much more often if they wish.

6.3 Work plan

The coordinator should keep a definitive version of the work plan. Since this plan will be maintained cooperatively (i.e. through heterarchical rather than hierarchical decision procedures), it should perhaps be accompanied by some rules about who is allowed to modify what.

6.4 Confidentiality

Since part of the coordinator's job is to disseminate information, the database should specify what each person is obliged to know, allowed to know, and forbidden to know. (Presumably this will be done through general assertions such as "People of category X are forbidden access to information of category Y.")

6.5 Progress reports

As explained above, the coordinator will need tools for designing report forms, ensuring that they are sent to the right people for compilation, collating the results, assessing reliability, comparing reports both with one another and with the work plan, and preparing global progress reports for the consortium directors. Many of these documents will have to be integrated into a database representing the history of the project.

6.6 Inferring how to find someone

So far we have considered only tools for collecting and organising information. We now consider ways in which this information might be used for automatic inference.

A simple expert system might use information about a person's plans, habits, duties, in order to suggest where to find him/her. For instance: "According to the work plan, X should spend this week doing task Y. Most of task Y is carried out at location Z, which can be reached by telephone 02-12345 or fax 02-12346."

6.7 Inferring who could carry out a task

Suppose that the coordinator must find at short notice a person or team that can perform an urgent task. Given a specification of the skills required, and the deadline, the system might search the database intelligently and find a team that is not only able to do the job, but has enough time (e.g. because it is currently working on a less urgent task).

6.8 Inferring who can provide knowledge

Often people are blocked for hours or days because they need a simple item of information but do not know who to ask. If participants are encouraged to provide detailed profiles of their knowledge and skills, a simple expert system could ask a few questions about the problem and then provide a list of people to ask (taking into account not only knowledge but also availability and level of responsibility - small queries should not be addressed to top management no matter how well they know the topic). Such a facility would be especially useful in projects involving several organisations, since it would facilitate unpredictable contacts across companies.

6.9 Inferring the consequences of a change in plan

If a delay is reported, the coordinator should be able to determine the consequences for the whole project. Normal project management software will suffice for this purpose, but it should be adapted for cooperative use. For instance, one might allow each team to alter details of the work plan within its responsibility; or one might allow the team to explore the global consequences of several alternative local modifications so that it can judge which is best.

6.10 Inferring who should receive documents

Given a formal specification of the content and purpose of each document, the system should be able to apply its knowledge about confidentiality and interests (see point 4) in order to distribute the document automatically to the appropriate people - or at least to prepare a mailing list which the coordinator can correct. This facility would save the coordinator some boring work compiling lists by hand. It might also prevent mistakes, for instance by reminding the coordinator that X should be informed of all decisions about topic Y. Perhaps all communications (not just those sent or received by the coordinator) should be checked to ensure that they do not violate confidentiality regulations.

7. Conclusions

A general framework for integrating CDPS into active CSCW has been proposed. The framework allows the design of systems with different degrees of human and computer participation as a realistic way to approach the design of cooperative distributed problem-solving architectures. An important problem in this type of system is user acceptability; the approach therefore stresses the gradual introduction of cooperative task facilitation along with the possibility of modifying the cooperation rules allowed by the knowledge base. To facilitate implementation of such systems a task-based software environment and a general methodology have been suggested.

6 Architectural framework for CSCW

Encarna Pastor, Jonny Jager

1. Previous approaches to CSCW architecture

1.1 Introduction

Although CSCW is a young research field, a multiplicity of paradigms, models, tools and applications already exist. Within their domains these have proved useful. However, comprehensive user support requires a pluralistic approach with the integration of different applications and current technologies. Since previous systems have been designed to support particular areas of functionality they usually lack integration.

In the present project we aim to identify a general integrated system architecture as a platform able to support all aspects of cooperative tasks. More specifically our objectives are as follows.

- To consider some contexts which determine the requirements for a common framework to support CSCW applications, and the relationships to other works in different fields.

- To present a set of concepts for CSCW system architecture and integration, so that effective use can be made of technology that supports collaboration independent of distance and time zones, thus increasing productivity.

- To analyse the properties required by the infrastructure which will support CSCW applications.

1.2 Motivation

In the absence of a general architectural framework for building distributed CSCW systems, much designer effort has been duplicated. Currently different application domains are covered by different applications from different vendors who have no common framework in which to establish a common agreed technology base. There is no opportunity to integrate the technologies used in the domains of computing, communications and networks.

It is important to stress that the scope of the problem is wider than that of mere communications interworking, which can be solved by the OSI reference model and standard protocols. Integration of CSCW applications requires attention to issues such as information, processing, communications, distribution, management, administration, specification, human factors, and the application environment itself. While currently these aspects are handled separately, what is required is a generic architectural approach which treats them all as facets of a single problem.

Some initial considerations affecting CSCW systems are the following:
- The distributed nature of CSCW applications;
- Concurrent access to resources;
- Addressing schemas and mobility;
- The use of different media (text, graphics, voice,...) over high speed digital networks;
- The need for compatibility with existing tools and applications;
- The impact of new organizational structures (e.g. pancake);
- The compression techniques needed.

1.3 Integrated architecture

The integration of different CSCW environment components in a common architectural framework will allow people and computers to utilize the underlying technology effectively. The common architectural framework must be more than a set of tools. It must be defined as a set of functional capabilities, so as to facilitate collaborative tasks by taking advantage of a broad set of resources.

Identification of an integrated architecture can begin by addressing the appropriate system to take advantage of existing applications and infrastructure. It should focus on the interfaces between applications, the enhancements and modifications required to make tools fully accessible, and the degree to which the tools work together to support collaborative tasks. Examples of available technologies include the following:
- Electronic mail
- Multimedia mail
- Electronic file transfer
- Directory services
- Remote access

- Shared files
- Database access
- Graphics presentation and storage
- Access Control and Authentication
- Structured interaction support.

Integration of technologies will lead to the definition of high-level functions, which would allow the evolution and enhancements of the current tools. Some advanced technologies like hypermedia and intelligent agents should probably be added to this list.

1.4 Some approaches

This section will review some suggested architectural models for CSCW. Although these proposals are in a very early stage, they are worth describing as a basis for discussion.

WG3-COST 14: Figure 6.1 shows a CSCW architectural model proposed by the Working Group 3 of the Co-Tech project (sponsored by COST 14).

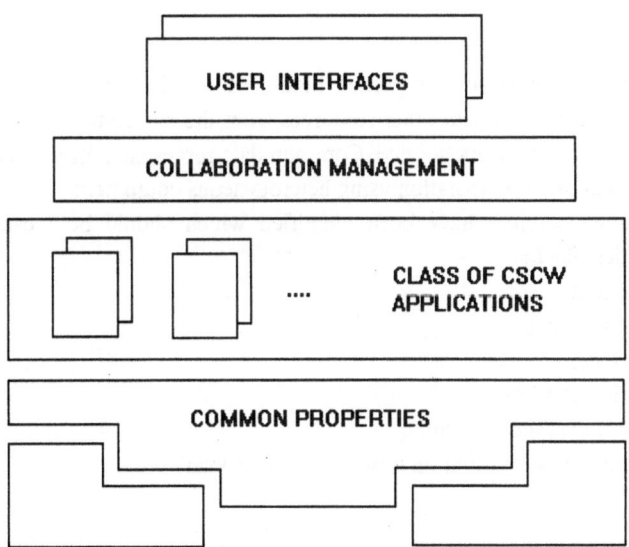

Figure 6.1 An architectural model for CSCW

The model consists of four main groups of building blocks (Kalin et al, 1990).

(i) The "user interfaces" represent a set of interfaces to adapt common information presentation to the specific needs and abilities of each particular user.

(ii) The "collaboration management" building block comprises all management functions which are common to all applications. For example:
- Conference timetable coordination
- Setup procedures (instant, asynchronous, centralized, distributed)
- Floor control
- Change of roles
- Conference suspension and restart
- Surveillance.

(iii) "CSCW application" is a basic building block needed for computer supported collaboration. Several applications have been identified:
- informal communication
- brainstorming
- chatting
- editing
- presentation
- remote control
- voting
- mail.

(iv) The role of the "common properties block" is to hide the heterogeneity of communication infrastructure and other resources from the application, and to offer it some kind of intelligent network service. Common data representation is to be defined on this level. This allows collaboration using heterogeneous equipment.
    Some important services have been identified which should be located in the common properties block:
- directory services
- resource management
- multicast services
- synchronization services
- "log" facility for session recording
- filtering/screening of information (information overload)

MultiG: MultiG is a collaborative research programme on distributed multimedia applications in a multi-gigabit per second network, carried on by several institutions in Sweden for the development of experimental high-speed networks and distributed multimedia applications (MultiG, 1991). The technical aim of the MultiG project is the design of multi-gigabps networks together with multimedia workstations which could be used as hosts that utilize the full power of the available bandwidth, and applications which match the human ability to communicate through several sense modalities.

Figures 6.2 and 6.3 show two relevant proposals on communication system architecture and computer system architecture.

The high speed networks will form a platform for distributed computing. In between distributed communicating user processes and the high speed network there are several layers of protocols. One of the MultiG projects aims to design a computer system architecture which can meet the high bandwidth requirements of distributed multimedia applications.

1.5 Open distributed processing (ODP)

Work on distributed processing in ISO started several years ago. The work on a reference model for ODP aims to provide the necessary structural framework for standardization on open distributed processing (ODP Reference Model, 1990). Some relevant concepts of ODP are explaining briefly in this section.

To construct models of ODP the first step is to abstract the properties common to all possible distributed systems and to express the requirements relevant to distributed processing of all possible enterprises. By investigating these properties an understanding of ODP can be gained. Some suggested properties are:
 - location/isolation
 - explicit communication/implicit communication/co operation
 - concurrency/parallel execution/ordering
 - incremental change/dynamic configuration/heterogeneity
 - multiple authority/autonomy property
 - partial failure/fault tolerance.

To derive an architecture, the ODP Reference Model standard group studied current practice and research in distributed computing and system design techniques. The study revealed that different experts have different viewpoints about what are the crucial concerns that make up distributed processing. Five viewpoints are dominant. A distributed system can be described in any one of these viewpoints or projections and the resulting descriptions or models reveal different facets of the system.

Each model is self-contained and complete. The difference between models lies not in how much of the system they describe, but rather in which aspects of the system they emphasize. Thus each viewpoint contains within it some abstraction of each of the other viewpoints. The purpose of the viewpoints is to provide a framework of abstractions. By partitioning the concerns to be addressed when describing all facets of an ODP system, the task is made simpler. The following scheme gives an overview of the five viewpoints and their areas of concern.

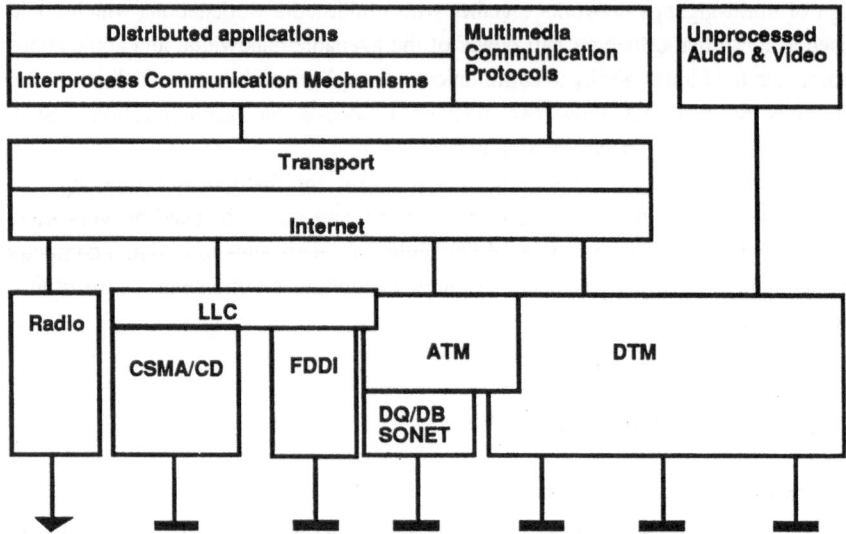

Figure 6.2 Communication system architecture

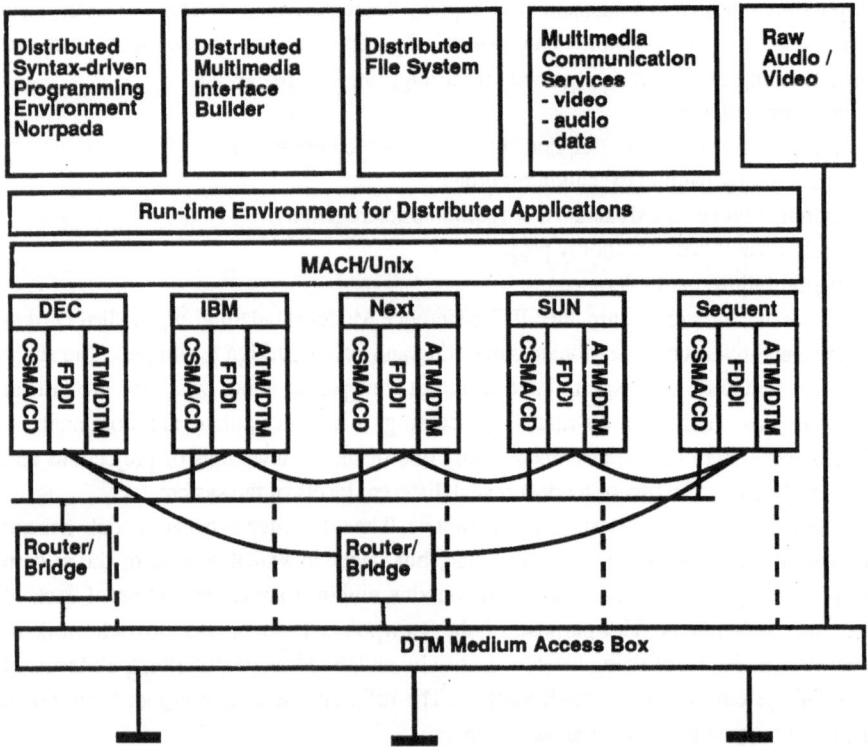

Figure 6.3 Computer system architecture

Enterprise viewpoint

Disciplines: Management, Ergonomics, Social sciences.

Areas of concern: Human and social issues, Management and finance, Legal.

What is specified: Requirements.

Information viewpoint

Disciplines: Data modelling, Knowledge representation (data models).

Areas of concern: Information modelling, Information flow, Information structure.

What is specified: Conceptual design and specifications.

Computation viewpoint

Disciplines: Software engineering.

Areas of concern: Application and process design and development (concurring models, ADTs, distributed algorithms, etc.).

What is specified: Design and development.

Engineering viewpoint

Disciplines: Operating systems, database systems, communication systems.

Areas of concern: Distributed system infrastructure, Application support (Transparencies, naming, binding, etc.).

What is specified: Infrastructure building blocks.

Technology viewpoint

Disciplines: End-products of relevant disciplines.

Areas of concern: Technological constraints.

What is specified: Technological constraints.

2. Functions of the support environment

2.1 Introduction

Our main objective is to identify a general integrated system architecture that will support all aspects of cooperative computer-mediated work. As a starting point we assume a view of the CSCW support environment represented in figure 6.4.

The support environment can be seen as a platform providing a set of high functional capabilities for users and applications, with access to a broad set of resources. Given this initial (and very simple) assumption, the following issues need to be addressed:

- Abstract definition of a generic architecture for the support environment, independent of the underlying technology, systems and implementations.
- Identification of the functionality that the support environment or platform must offer to its users (humans and applications).
- Identification of the requirements from the underlying infrastructure that the platform must satisfy (multimedia, broadband communication, mobility, etc.).
- Instantiation of the abstract architecture - that is, definition of the correspondence between architectural abstract concepts and "real" resources in a distributed computer system.

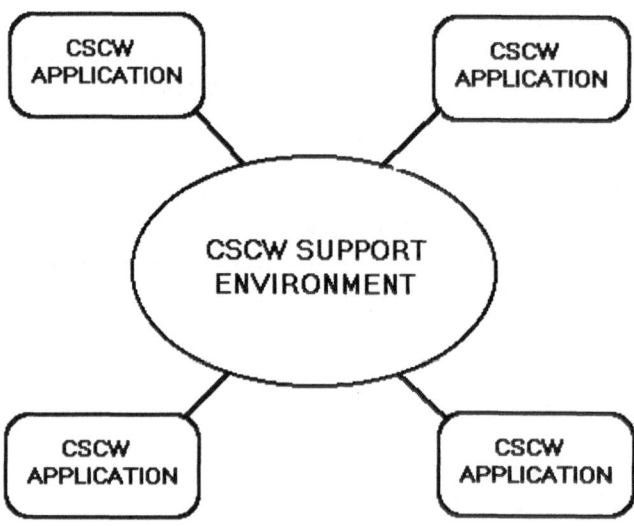

Figure 6.4 A simple CSCW architecture

The rest of this section focusses on the second item, namely functionality.

2.2 CSCW requirements

To determine the functions that the support environment for CSCW applications must offer, the requirements of potential users must be identified and analysed in detail. From the descriptions and models of the cases studies presented in chapters 3 and 4, the following list of requirements has been compiled. Although the list is neither complete nor accurate, it serves as a starting point for the identification of a set of common support functions (these will be presented in the next section).

Activity management
- parallel activities
- serial activities

Activity coordination (Facilitator)
- Monitoring and surveillance
Design of report forms
- joint editing
- annotations/comments on documents

Evaluation of reports

Confidentiality, security, access control

Time management

Scheduling meetings

Resource allocation
- who will carry out a task
- who will provide knowledge

Storage of information (database)
- tasks, activities, work plan
- people, responsibilities, etc.
- history of the project
- corporate directory, global directory

Communication
- Conferencing
    support for roles
    topics
- Dissemination of information, conclusions, suggestions, documents,...
- Interpersonal communication
    distribution list
- Communications in groups
    synchronous, asynchronous, across companies
- News, bulletin boards, circulars, ...

Presentation of information to the user
- windows
- multimedia interfaces (audio, video, text, graphics, ...)
- intelligent agents/assistants, WYSIWIS, etc.

2.3 Functions of the support environment

Bearing in mind the requirements listed above, and taking the classification schema being proposed in the ODP Reference Model (1990), the following set of general/common functions can be identified.

User access
- Device control
- Representation (format)
- Presentation ("look", window manipulation)
- Multimedia operation
- Views of the information (semantic)
- Transparency of the information location
- Cultural selection

Storage of information
- Data manipulation
    create, destroy, examine
    modify, compare, combine
- Schema management
- Translation between data models
- Access control, concurrency control, transactions

Processing (information transformation)
- Invocation of processes for execution
    Initiate, terminate activities
    enable, disable execution
    suspend, resume activities
- Synchronization/ordering of the execution
    Time synchronization
    Transaction processing control
    Interactions
- Client/server and producer/consumer computational roles

Communication
- Electronic mail (interpersonal), distribution lists
- File and document transfer
- News services
- conference

Identification (naming)
- Registration, binding, publication
- Trading (establishing contracts between objects that use service

and those that provide them)
- Directories
- Dictionaries

Management
- Scheduling, coordination and maintenance of resources in the environment
  These are the management functions required by the support
  environment itself. It must provide mechanisms enabling
  components of the environment to be monitored and controlled.
  The managed components may be (distributed) applications,
  computer systems, networks, user roles, connections, services,
  i.e. resources in general.
- Maintenance of relationships between managing and/or managed objects.
- Maintenance of monitoring activities
- Collection of statistical information, accounting
- Date and time management
- Event handling
- Configuration functions
- Resource sharing

Security
- Authentication
- Authorisation
- Cryptographic support.

3. Proposal for a CSCW architecture

3.1 Introduction

In general, the concept of Cooperative Work (CW) designates specific cooperative relations, characterized by shared responsibilities; cooperation can be seen as the planned work of a group of interacting people. Most such interactions are based on or accompanied by communication. Consequently, to support cooperation we should provide facilities that are useful both for private work and for interaction.

Computer support (CS) implies that these facilities are provided by computer systems which support different aspects of individual and collective work.

Today, from the user's point of view, the performing of computer-based cooperative work can be an extremely complex and exasperating experience. The systems currently available have been designed to support specialised areas of functionality, and lack integration. A comprehensive user support requires a pluralistic approach and the integration of different cooperative work requirements.

The role of computer technology must consist first of all in ensuring that the computer does not *disrupt* the collective activity that is already in progress (Bannon & Schmidt 1991). Furthermore, with regard to CS, the goal is to support existing cooperative work rather than to construct systems that make cooperation possible.

In the strongest sense, this has led to many systems which support a number of applications that are in fact unable to cooperate. This is the typical state of the art today (Kuna & Klehn, 1991). On the other hand, from the point of view of system designers, no general architectural framework has been defined for building distributed CSCW systems, so that much design work is duplicated. At present, different application domains are covered by different applications from different vendors with no common technological basis. Integration of CSCW applications requires attentionn to such issues as information, processing, communication, distribution, management, administration, specification, human factors, and the application environment itself. Although currently these aspects are dealt with separately, what is needed is a generic architectural approach which treats them all as facets of a single problem. This is the approach adopted in this project: solutions are derived from analysis of two major domains - technology on the one hand, and psychology, organisation, and management on the other.

3.2 The technology solution

In accordance with the methodology just described, technological aspects must be addressed through the following steps:

- Identify a generic architectural framework to support cooperative computer-mediated work, and define the environment where the architecture is to be used.

- Specify the set of components which make up the architectural framework. We will suggest a specific architecture from which specific solutions can be configured.

3.2.1 Architectural framework

The identification of an architecture could be affected by assumptions about the context where it will be applied. As a starting point, the following *properties* have been considered.
- The distributed nature of CW, and hence of the CSCW applications.
- The need for concurrent access to shared resources.
- The use of different media (text, graphics, voice, etc.) over (high speed) digital networks.

- The need to establish compatibility with existing tools and applications.
- The possibility of managing both synchronous and asynchronous styles of collaboration.

Figure 6.5 gives an overview of the building blocks of the proposed architecture.

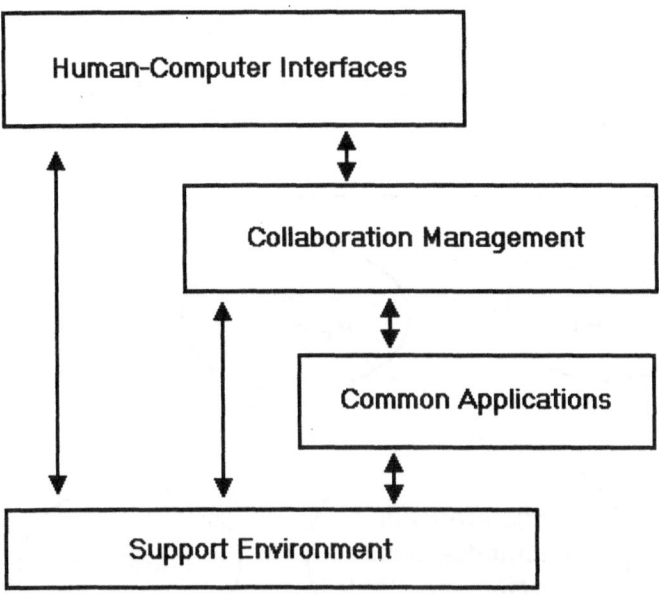

Figure 6.5 A proposed CSCW architecture

3.2.2 Human-computer interface

The set of interfaces must provide a common style of information presentation which can be adapted to the specific needs and abilities of individual users. It should also provide mechanisms which facilitate the use of the collaborative tools offered by the system.

3.2.3 Collaboration management

The components in this building block form a shared controlled environment where applications are executed. They could be considered as the specific part of a given CSCW application, although the generic/abstract definition of the components is common to every application. Different applications will produce different instancaes of these components.

The *Role Agent* (see figure 6.6) is the entity assuming knowledge about the cooperative activity to be performed. It has a set of obligations and methods (see chapter 5) as well as cooperation procedures to permit effective interaction with other Role Agents (Danielsen & Pastor, 1988).

The *Activity Manager* is the component responsible for the coordination, control, scheduling, monitoring, and tuning, of the activities currently being carried out by the network of Role Agents.

The *Facilitator* can be considered as the mediator agent, performing coordination and monitoring tasks between different activities (perhaps in different enterprises).

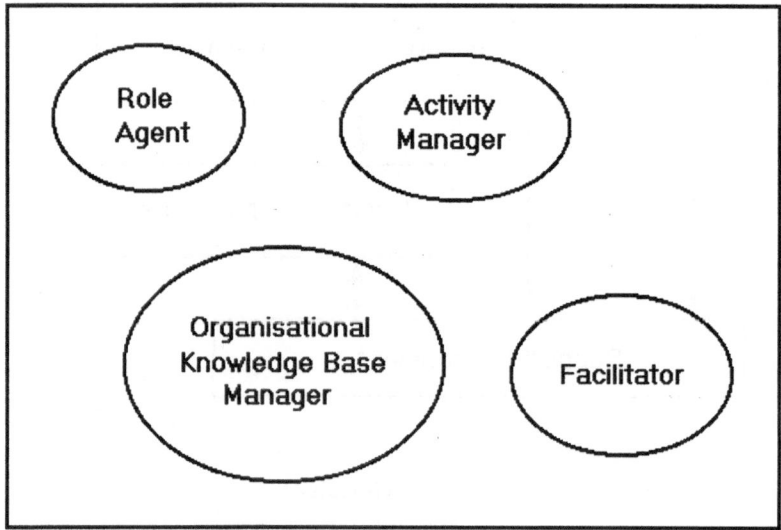

Figure 6.6 Collaboration management

The *Organisational Knowledge Base Manager* is the component taking care of the shared information about organisational resources, relationships, dependencies, and constraints (management information base).

3.2.4 Common applications

In this building block reside those applications which have been recognised as common for a broad set of CSCW applications (figure 6.7).

The components in the Collaboration Management block will make use of the facilities provided by the common applications. Specially relevant for our purposes are the Conference, Interpersonal Communications, and Document Library applications.

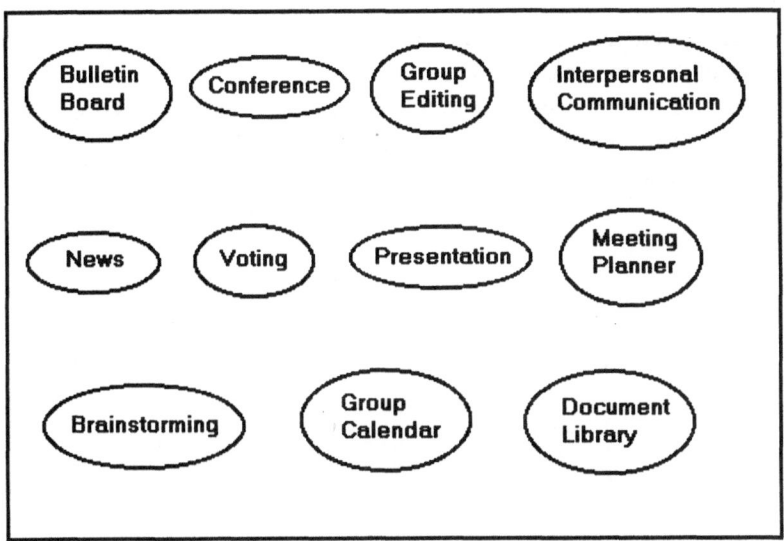

Figure 6.7 Common applications

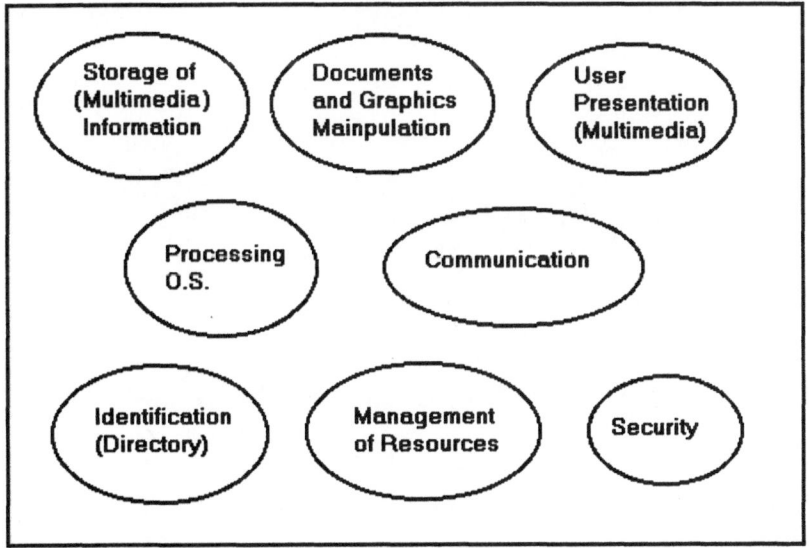

Figure 6.8 Support environment

3.2.5 Support environment/platform

This consists of system components which provide applications with a set of high functional capabilities and access to a broad set of system resources (figure 6.8). The functionality of these components has been outlined in section 2.

The platform also provides applications and users with facilities for isolating themselves from distribution and the heterogeneity of systems, services, and communication networks.

7 A methodology for CSCW

Richard Power, Mike Martin

In this final chapter we summarize our conclusions, first about the commercial significance of CSCW for organizations, and second about the methods by which effective CSCW products will be developed.

1. The significance of CSCW for organizations

The term "cooperative work" refers to any situation in which people act together to achieve shared goals. The people who are collaborating may be located in the same building, so that they can meet face to face. Alternatively, they may be located in different buildings, cities, or countries, perhaps because they belong to separate organizations; in this case, communication may be synchronous (e.g. a telephone call) or asynchronous (e.g. a telefax message). The emerging field of Computer Supported Cooperative Work (CSCW) aims to facilitate collaboration in all these contexts.

There are strong grounds for thinking that CSCW will become a key technology during the 1990s. Numerous studies have reported a movement towards greater flexibility in organizing work. Members of a project team no longer work in the same office, during the same hours, under strict centralised control. There exists moreover a worldwide trend (especially marked in Europe) towards the formation of joint ventures and consortia for large-scale technical projects. As a result, individuals and groups from different organizations, often located in different countries, may have to collaborate intensively, exchanging messages or engaging in synchronous communication not just occasionally but almost every day.

Intensive research on CSCW dates from the early 1980s; the first full conference was held in 1986. Although the obvious promise of the field has attracted some leading researchers, the experimental systems developed so far have had little commercial impact. Most existing CSCW applications are stand-alone tools which originated from some new technical idea (e.g. the idea of using speech-act theory in order to design semi-structured messages). The crucial flaw in this procedure is that a solution is proposed without first defining the problem. To develop effective CSCW tools we must begin by investigating the contexts in which cooperative work occurs. In most work contexts there are complex networks of communication, linked to complex distributions of power and responsibility. Any serious attempt to model a cooperative enterprise requires a prolonged study using appropriate specialized methods.

The second major prerequisite for effective CSCW is the integration of tools into a common environment. All CSCW applications include some basic functions like the storage and display of documents. Without a common framework these functions have to be realised anew for each application; this means not only that effort is duplicated, but that a special interface has to be created every time we want to link two applications together, so that for example a document created by one system can be read by another. With many functions already supported by a common environment, any new CSCW tool can be developed much more rapidly, and integration with existing applications becomes virtually automatic.

In synthesis, we propose an improved methodology for the development of CSCW applications, comprising the following points.
(i) Analysis of cooperative enterprises, with the aim of discovering areas where support is needed.
(ii) Identification of common functions required by CSCW systems and design of a suitable environment.
(iii) Design and implementation of a set of tools to support cooperative work.

In the PECOS project we have studied two cases: the construction of a high-speed train for the Italian state railway, and the creation of an integrated information system for environmental protection in the Lombardy region. These studies have drawn attention to some issues of current concern in the coordination of large-scale projects.

If a project is badly coordinated, delivery of the final product will be delayed. In domains of slow technological evolution such delays may do little damage; but in domains of rapid technical advance, where novel products appear often, any company which reaches the market a few months after its competitors will obtain a drastically reduced share. This phenomenon has been called "time-based competition". Because of time-based competition, it is vital that projects at the leading edge of technology should be managed effectively. However, precisely for projects of this type, traditional methods of management often work poorly. Advanced technological projects typically present problems of *unpredictability* (the product specification and work plan cannot be stated definitively at the outset) and *contemporaneity* (many interdependent subtasks are performed in parallel). As a result, unexpected problems repeatedly occur which call for rapid modifications in the product specifications or work plan. The traditional management hierarchy is too slow to cope with this kind of complexity. What seems to be needed is a heterarchical style of management, in which some decisions are taken through conferences among technicians rather than being passed up to a higher level.

These points can be illustrated with reference to some problems encountered during the first case study, the construction of a high-speed train. Although a prototype of the train had been built, the complete product required further innovations, so the design and the work plan could not be fully specified in advance. The work was distributed among four constructor companies; although obliged to collaborate in the context of the train project, these companies were market competitors, hence their loyalties were sometimes divided. Technicians were reluctant to report delays, or to give realistic estimates, through fear of their company losing face. When decisions required consultation between technicians from different companies, the relevant people were either not in touch, or uncertain of their powers and duties, or uncertain whether or how their decision should be communicated to others. Decisions were taken without their underlying rationale being discussed or even recorded.

The following case illustrates the sort of unexpected situation that might cause delay. X works at a factory in Naples, producing a motor; Y works for a different company in Milan, producing the framework into which the motor and other components should be assembled. Since the exact shape of the motor could not be specified in advance, Y cannot build and test the relevant part of the framework until X finishes the motor and sends it to Milan. Owing to a defect in his original design, X is obliged to modify the form of the motor and to deliver it two weeks late. He might report this problem to his project manager so that it could be raised next week at a meeting of the coordinating committee; however, the matter could be sorted out better and more quickly by getting directly in touch with Y. Ideally the conversation might proceed thus:

X: I've had to modify the motor. There will be a delay of two weeks.

Y: But that means I can't finish the framework.

X: Can't you use the two weeks to do something else?

Y: No, I can't fit the wiring and other attachments until I know the shape of the motor. Can you build a maquette which simulates the motor and send me that?

X: Yes, but it will delay me another three days.

Y: Never mind, the priority now is to build the framework.

This conversation can occur only if some conditions are satisfied. First, X must realize that his problem with the motor has global consequences. Next, he must know that the problem can and should be resolved by consulting another technician - i.e. through lateral rather than vertical consultation. He must know how to get in touch with Y, and have an effective means of exchanging messages. Ideally the negotiation should be accessible at least to some other interested parties. For instance Z, the person responsible for testing the mechanical properties of the motor, might have something to say about the extra three-day delay due to constructing the maquette. Perhaps the decision should have been taken by a larger group including Z.

This example shows that it would be inadequate merely to provide X and Y with a means of communication, such as the telephone or electronic mail. What they need most of all is guidance on how to proceed, not from their managers but from an independent agent whose job is to facilitate the whole project. One important task for CSCW will be to provide tools to support the facilitator in promoting and administering appropriate conferences between people working in different organizations and at different geographical locations.

2. A methodology for developing CSCW applications

In designing any application, it is important to separate the activity of *describing the problem* from that of *formulating a solution*. Many current methods of system analysis fail because the problem is described through concepts that correspond directly to a preferred set of solution components: in effect, the problem owner is forced to state the problem in terms of a technological solution. This prevents the effective exploration of alternative solutions, except within narrow bounds, and leaves many policies and requirements implicit or expressed only indirectly. Perhaps even more significantly, it fails to allow for the fact that a solution may change the problem, by causing some evolution or transformation of the user organization.

The correct approach, in our view, is to employ distinct conceptual frameworks for stating problems and stating solutions. When this approach is adopted, the transition from problem to solution cannot be performed mechanically, because the problem is described in terms that admit not just one but many possible solutions, so that to reach a decision several candidates must be evaluated.

In the PECOS project we have focussed on a particular domain of problem and solution, that of the cooperative coordination of complex organizations. The definition of a problem in this domain necessarily includes multiple interested parties - the cooperating enterprises; the conceptual framework for articulating the problem must be rich enough to express the relationships between functions and resources, and also the obligations and responsibilities associated with cooperative behaviour.

Solutions for this domain derive from two broad fields: first, technology and engineering; second, psychology and management. Thus a CSCW solution cannot be regarded merely as a set of software tools: it includes as well a social or organizational aspect. For example, a tool enabling a facilitator to organize an asynchronous conference among people at remote locations cannot be used effectively unless the appropriate organizational procedures, rights, and duties, have been established. Thus our repertory of solution components for CSCW should include psychological, social and organizational components as well as technical/engineering ones.

Figure 7.1 depicts the key aspects of our methodology, distinguishing the problem definition, the technological solution, and the organizational solution. Each aspect requires its own characteristic methods. The diagram does not imply any particular ordering of activities; in practice the process is iterative. The roles of problem owner, problem analyst, and solution architect, are implicit: the application of the method will be reflected in the dialogue that takes place between them.

In the solution domain we include two sources of knowledge and procedures for problem solving: first, the people participating in the work; second, the intelligent tools provided by the CSCW system. These sources will overlap, in the sense that they have some knowledge and procedures in common. By this means, the system promotes the rapid creation and maintenance of reliable shared cognitive models among the users, and so helps to ensure that local decisions take account of global consequences.

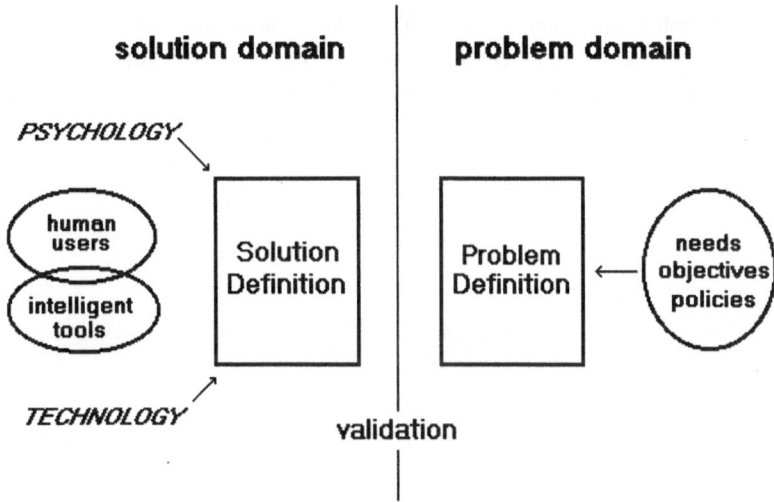

Figure 7.1 Summary of the proposed methodology

We envisage that problems will be defined through the following steps.
(i) Elicit and collect statements of need and policy.
(ii) Express these statements in an appropriate problem definition language.
(iii) Show these reformulated descriptions to the problem owners, and revise them until consensus is reached.
(iv) Identify, specify, and justify the implied functional requirements.
Although here presented sequentially, these steps will in practice be performed iteratively, so that for example the original statements in free text will be revised after

the problem owners have discussed their reformulations in the problem definition language.

The elements of a solution architecture are as follows:

(i) Definition of the application domain, and the sort of needs and policies which it is designed to address.

(ii) Specification of the components from which a solution may be configured.

(iii) Rules for combining these components - these constitute the solution engineering discipline.

(iv) Recommendations, guidelines, and examples of good engineering practice. To create interesting solutions we need powerful components flexibly combined. If the rules of combination permit only safe, well-behaved solutions, experience shows that they will also be of little value or interest.

As already emphasized, the proposed method defines roles and responsibilities for people as well as providing tools and procedures. Thus, on the psychological/social side of the solution domain we define components such as decision conferences, consensus mechanisms, and coordination roles. These are implemented at the organizational level. On the technology side we find such solution components as intelligent problem-solving models, distributed document conference shells, and common user interface managers.

Appendix: Catalogue of CSCW systems

Richard Power, Lorella Carminati

1. Argnoter

History: A tool for the Colab computerized meeting room. Resembles Cognoter but aims to reconcile conflicting proposals rather than to compose a joint document.

Features: Supports a "proposal meeting". There is a joint task (e.g. designing a product) on which participants have different positions. During the proposing phase, proposals are made explicit: as in Cognoter, each is represented by a label which can be expanded on request in several further windows. During the arguing phase people submit reasons for accepting or rejecting each proposal. Finally, there is an evaluation phase in which decision criteria are made explicit and an agreed proposal is constructed. New proposals can be quickly assembled from fragments of existing ones.

References: Stefik et al. 1987.

2. Callisto

History: Started at the Digital Equipment Corporation (DEC) in 1981. Originally an expert system for project management, designed for a single user. Second phase adapted the system to multiple users, each with a Mini-Callisto.

Features: Resembles standard PM software in that it supports scheduling and resource management. Each user can define tasks and constraints ("project knowledge"); if the system detects inconsistencies among these assertions it tries to resolve them through "constraint-directed negotiation".

References: Sathi et al. 1986.

3. Caucus

History: Produced by Metasystems Design Group Inc (VA). Runs on mainframe and IBM-PC. Supports conferences of up to 16 users. Used at 100 sites including Boeing Defence and Space Systems.

Features: Contributions may arrive at any time. Discussions on different topics are kept separate. Access to technical data base including definitions of key terms. Has been used for collecting comments on a product from many diverse sources.
References: Opper 1988.

4. Cognoter

History: A tool developed by Stefik and others for the Colab project at Xerox PARC. (Colab is an experimental computerised meeting room.) Cognoter helps co-authors to organise ideas.
Features: The meeting has three phases: brainstorming, organising, evaluating. During brainstorming ideas (short titles) are written on a shared window which serves as a chalkboard. They may be amplified by paragraphs of text, normally hidden but accessible by clicking a mouse. Complex ideas may be elaborated on separate chalkboards. During organising, arrows between ideas indicate which should come first. During evaluation, the whole structure is pruned and refined until it obtains general approval.
References: Stefik et al. 1987.

5. COKES

History: Experimental system developed at Carleton University by Kaye & Karam, using PROLOG.
Features: Uses information about office procedures in order to support office work. Features: Employs an intelligent agent architecture. Each user has an assistant (a computerised agent) that can perform actions or obtain information by interacting with the assistants of other users.
References: Kaye & Karam 1987.

6. CONFER

History: Developed at the University of Michigan in the middle 1970s by a group led by Merril Flood.
Features: Early conferencing system. Introduced idea of reply-oriented as opposed to time-oriented transcript, grouping contributions according to the topic sequence they belonged to rather than following chronological order. Also included a sophisticated preference-voting system to support group decision making.
References: Zinn et al. 1976.

7. Coordinator

History: Produced by Action Technologies (CA). Based on work by Winograd and Flores. Aims to facilitate computer-based conversations in work groups.

Features: Models typical conversations as speech act networks. Records the commitments implied by each speech act, so that users can be reminded of where they stand. Each contribution is located in a history of the conversation.
References: Winograd & Flores 1986, Winograd 1988.

8. Delphi conference

History: An early attempt to provide support for group problem solving by asynchronous communication, created in 1971.
Features: Based on the Delphi problem-solving method for complex unstructured problems, a precursor of the IBIS method.
References: Turoff 1972.

9. Diamond

History: Developed by Thomas (et al.) at BBN Laboratories (MA). Runs on LAN of workstations with accessories like image scanners and voice input/output devices. Permits users to create and send multimedia documents.
Features: Documents may contain text, diagrams, images (e.g. from a map or a photograph), recorded speech, and spread sheets. By clicking on an icon the receiver can hear the spoken message. If the receiver changes the data in the spread sheet, new results will be calculated by formulae or procedures specified by the author.
References: Thomas et al. 1985.

10. EIES

History: Electronic Information Exchange System. An early system for computer-mediated communication, operational in 1976.
Features: Supported messages, conferences, notebooks, an activity monitor, and a directory of members. Included a language called INTERACT which enabled tools to be developed quickly for specific contexts.
References: Johnson-Lenz et al. 1980.

11. EMISARI

History: Emergency Management Information System And Reference Index. Developed at the USA office of emergency preparedness in 1971 to support decision making during national emergencies.
Features: Allowed 100-200 people in different regions of the country to collaborate in crisis management. Data forms could be created and assigned to particular people who had to fill them in; the system kept track of such responsibilities. Messages could be attached to data, so that discussions might develop around crucial data items. Procedures could be defined so that the system would monitor the people responsible for executing them.
References: McKendree 1977.

12. ForComment

History: Produced by Broderburg Software (CA), based on work by Edwards and Levine. Supports up to 16 users on IBM-PCs. Intended for group editing of documents.
Features: Multiple reviewers may comment on a document, viewing and amplifying each other's remarks without altering the original version. Only the original author can decide whether to incorporate these comments. Document can be printed with or without comments. Comments can be indexed according to their source, so that one can see a list of all the changes proposed by any given person.
References: Opper 1988.

13. gIBIS

History: Developed at MCC Texas by Conklin and others around 1988. Permits user to construct and explore, through a graphical interface, diagrams which represent the discussion underlying a decision or plan. Runs on a SUN workstation.
Features: Based on the IBIS method which distinguishes issues, positions, and arguments. Experiments suggest that communication within a team improves if people are trained to organise their contributions according to this method.
References: Conklin et al. 1988.

14. Higgins

History: Produced by Conetic Systems (CA). Runs on IBM-PC with LAN (Local Area Network). Workgroup communication system.
Features: Built around relational database. Each user has keyword access to group calendars, shared project information, and a personal filing system. Includes E-mail, scheduling, project tracking, expense reporting, calculator, notepad, telephone dialer, passwords, and data security through encryption of all text files. A further optional facility will send messages by fax to anyone who cannot be reached by E-mail.
References: Opper 1988.

15. Information Lens

History: Developed by Malone (et al.) at MIT in the mid 1980s. Runs on Xerox workstations. Offered as "an intelligent system for information sharing in organisations".
Features: Basically like E-mail but with semi-structured messages, and services which exploit this structure. Helps user decide what information to convey; automatically organises incoming mail according to topic and priority; performs some automatic actions on the basis of the fixed- format information; suggests actions that users might perform.
References: Malone et al. 1987.

16. MERMAID

History: Developed by Watabe and others at NEC, Japan. Supports synchronous meetings among people at different locations.

Features: Multimedia interface including workstations, video cameras, audio link, image scanner, electronic writing pad. Each participant's face is filmed and may appear in windows on other workstations. Several people may talk at once. Information may be shared in public windows.

References: Watabe et al. 1990.

17. NLS/Augment

History: Developed from 1963-1976 by Douglas Engelbart and others at the Augmentation Research Centre (Stanford). Pioneered many ideas including windows, mouse.

Features: Real-time communication through shared windows. Organising and indexing documents, including ones produced in multiple versions, perhaps by different authors. Efficient maintenance and access to very large document libraries including texts generated both internally and externally. Computer-based instruction allowing novices to communicate with experts through a shared screen. Maintenance of a common work plan in project management.

References: Engelbart & English 1968; Engelbart & Lehtman 1988

18. Officetalk

History: Implemented at the Xerox Palo Alto Research Centre (PARC) in the late 1970s. Ran on a network of minicomputers. Aimed to facilitate document management, preparation, and communication.

Features: Standard display of four indices and a current document. The indices are called in-basket, out-basket, forms (saved documents), and blanks (documents to be prepared). Much attention to interface issues.

References: Ellis & Nutt 1980.

19. Office Works

History: Produced by Data Access Corp (FL) 1988. Designed to automate many kinds of office work.

Features: Messages (e.g. from telephone) may be sent by receptionist to the relevant people, with urgency index. Each user can receive, compose, file, send messages. Meetings automatically arranged if you specify who should attend and when the meeting should take place. Personal schedules of partipants are taken into account. Database of all business contacts. Messages may be routed to E-mail, telex or fax. Documents are indexed by owner, author, recipient, date, or keyword.

References: Opper 1988.

20. Omega

History: Developed by Barber at MIT. Supports office work.

Features: Each user can specify goals. The system evaluates whether goals are appropriate and feasible, taking into account the current situation and the goals of others. If not, it provides information enabling users to modify either their goals or the underlying constraints.

References: Barber 1981.

21. Polymer

History: Expert system for office work developed by Croft and Lefkowitz at University of Massachusetts.

Features: Based on AI planning theory. Can be used to support repetitive group tasks. Proposes a plan, monitors progress, and modifies the plan if necessary.

References: Croft & Lefkowitz 1988.

22. Régnier's Abacus

History: Developed by F. Régnier and P. Lybaert for the French company AIRELLE.

Features: A tool for displaying the attitudes of a group of people towards a set of issues. First a list of perhaps 30 statements is compiled. Beside each statement there is a grid of seven responses, coded by colour in a scheme resembling traffic lights (Green affirmative, Red negative, Orange neutral, White means "Can't answer", Black means "Won't answer"). Each member in the group of perhaps 20 people provides a response to each statement. The whole set of attitudes is displayed through a 20x30 grid in which single responses are represented by coloured rectangular pixels. Using this method of display, global trends and local patterns leap immediately to the eye.

23. SCOOP

History: System for Computerisation Of Office Processing, developed by Zisman in the late 1970s. Emphasis not on interface but on office procedures.

Features: Models the tasks of each agent (person or program) by Petri nets. Provides a language for creating models for any given office. Utilizes these models in order to carry out automated actions, or (presumably) to remind people to carry out non-automated actions.

References: Ellis & Nutt 1980.

24. SDSE

History: System Development Support Environment was developed by Kedsierski in the early 1980s. It provides a cooperative environment for developing applications with the CHI language.

Features: Permits communication through speech acts, the main categories being Question, Inform, Complain, Plan, Request. When an act is performed, the system not only sends the message but also performs other appropriate actions, asking for more information if necessary. For example, if someone complains about a bug, it might add the bug to a list, warn everybody, and look up who wrote the bugged code.
References: Kedziersky 1982.

25. SIBYL

History: Under development by Lee at MIT. Represents decision rationale.
Features: Resembles gIBIS but employs a richer formalism for representing discussion.
References: Lee 1990.

26. Strudel

History: Developed by Shepherd and others at the Hewlett-Packard Laboratories, Palo Alto, around 1990. Provides a toolkit for computerised conversation.
Features: Like the Coordinator, enhances E-mail by organising contributions into conversations, defined according to Speech Act theory. More flexible in that new conversational patterns can be defined by the user.
References: Shepherd et al. 1990.

27. SuperSync

History: Produced by SwixTech USA 1988. Based on research by Adams on group formation. Facilitates team development. Runs on IBM-PC.
Features: Analyses behaviour of company employees. Produces "sociograms" which show how each person view the group. Helps managers to put together an effective team. Predicts how any proposed set of people will work together as a group.
References: Opper 1988.

28. Visual Scheduler

History: Developed by Beard and others at North Carolina University. In use since 1987. Schedules group meetings.
Features: Each user represents his/her individual schedule by a table in which busy periods are black and free periods white. Superimposing these schedules, the coordinator can distinguish periods when most people are free (light grey) or busy (dark grey).
References: Beard et al. 1990.

29. WordPerfect Office

History: Produced by WordPerfect Corp (UT). Can run on LAN of PCs. Originated from requests by the US Department of Justice; used by some law firms.

Features: Provides normal editing, messaging, and scheduling tools with access to E-mail. A file manager helps organise data files and programs in local and network directories. A shell program directs traffic among applications, so that any activity can be interrupted by another. For instance, there is no need to close down work on editing a document in order to consult your calendar or address book.

References: Opper 1988.

References

Alonso M., Cuena J., Molina M. (1990) SIRAH: An architecture for a professional intelligence. Proceedings 9th European Conference on Artificial Intelligence ECAI-90. Pitman.

Austin, J.L. (1962) How to do things with words. Oxford University Press.

Bannon, L.J. & Schmidt, K. (1991) Four characters in search of a context. In Bowers, J.M. & Benford, S.D. (ed) Studies in Computer Supported Cooperative Work. North-Holland, Elsevier Science Publishers B.V.

Barber, G.R. (1981) Supporting organizational problem solving with a workstation. In Limb, J.O. (ed) Proceedings supplement of the conference on office information systems. ACM, Philadelphia PA, 33-44.

Baron, R.A. (1986) Behaviour in organizations: understanding and managing the human side of work. Allyn & Bacon Inc., Boston.

Beard, D., Murugappan, P., Humm, A., Banks, D., Nair, A. & Shan, Y-P. (1990) A visual calendar for scheduling group meetings. In Bikson, T.K. Proceedings of the conference on computer supported cooperative work, Los Angeles. ACM Press, New York.

Benne, K.D. & Sheats, P. (1948) Functional roles of group members. Journal of social issues 4, 41-49.

Bikson, T.K. (ed) (1990) Proceedings of the conference on computer supported cooperative work, Los Angeles. ACM Press, New York.

Bond, A.H. & Gasser, L. (eds) (1988) Readings in distributed artificial intelligence. Morgan Kaufmann, San Mateo CA.

Brothers L., Sembugamoorthy V., & Muller M. (1990) ICICLE: Groupware for code inspection. In Bikson, T.K. Proceedings of the conference on computer supported cooperative work, Los Angeles. ACM Press, New York.

Brown D.C., Chandrasekaran B. (1989) Design problem solving. Pitman, Morgan Kaufmann.

Bullen, C.V. & Bennett, J.L. (1990) Learning from user experience with groupware. In Bikson, T.K. Proceedings of the conference on computer supported cooperative work, Los Angeles. ACM Press, New York.

Burgess, K.C. & Conklin, J. (1990) Report on a development project use of an issue-based information system. In Bikson, T.K. Proceedings of the conference on computer supported cooperative work, Los Angeles. ACM Press, New York.

Cammarata, S., McArthur, S. & Steeb, R. (1983) Strategies for cooperation in distributed problem solving. Proc IJCAI-83. Morgan Kaufmann.

Chandrasekaran B. (1983) Towards a taxonomy of problem solving types. A.I. Magazine 4:1, 9-17.

Chandrasekaran, B. (1986) Generic tasks in knowledge based reasoning: high level building blocks for expert systems design. IEEE Expert.

Cohen, P.R. & Perrault, C.R. (1979) Elements of a plan-based theory of speech acts. Cognitive Science 3, 177-212.

Conklin, J. & Begeman, M. (1988) gIBIS: a tool for exploratory policy discussion. ACM Transactions on Office Information Systems (TOOIS) October 1988.

Corkill, D. (1979) Hierarchical planning in a distributed environment. Proc IJCAI-79, Morgan Kaufmann.

Corkil, D. & Lesser, V.R. (1983) The use of metalevel control for coordination in a distributed problem solving network. Proc IJCAI-83, Morgan Kaufmann.

Croft, W.B. & Lefkowitz, L.S. (1988) Using a planner to support office work. In Allen, R.B. (ed) Proceedings of the conference on office automation systems. Palo Alto CA, ACM Press, 55-62.

Cuena J. (1991) Intelligent systems for traffic flow management: a qualitative modelling approach. International Journal of Intelligent Systems.

Cuena J., Garrote L., Molina M. (1991) An architecture for cooperation of knowledge bases and quantitative models: the CYRAH environment. XI International Workshop on Expert Systems. Special conference on Second Generation Expert Systems Avignon. EC2 Press, Nanperre.

Danielsen, T. & Pastor, E. (1988) Cooperating intelligent agents. In Speth, R. (ed) Research into networks and distributed applications. North-Holland.

Davis, R. & Smith, R.G. (1983) Negotiation as a metaphor for distributed problem solving. Artificial Intelligence 20(1).

Durfee, E.H. (1988) Coordination of distributed problem sovers. Kluwer.

Durfee, E.H. & Lesser, V.R. (1987) Using partial global plans to coordinate distributed problem solvers. Proc IJCAI-87, Morgan Kaufmann.

Durfee, E.H., Lesser, V.R. & Corkill, D. (1989) Cooperative distributed problem solving. In Barr, A., Cohen, A.P., & Feigenbaum, E. (eds) Handbook of artificial intelligence, Chapter XVII. Addison-Wesley.

Ellis, C. & Nutt, G. (1980) Office information systems and computer science. Computing surveys 12(1), 27-60.

Engelbart, D. & English, W. (1968) A research center for augmenting human intellect. Proceedings of FJCC 33(1) 395-410 AFIPS Press, Montvale NY.

Engelbart, D. & Lehtman, H. (1988) Working together. BYTE December 245-252.

Feldman, D.C. (1984) The development and enforcement of group norms. Academy of management review 9, 47-53.

Fikes R.E., Hart P.E., Nilsson N. (1972) Learning and executiong generalized robot plans. Artificial Intelligence 3:4, 251-288.

Garfinkel, H. (1967) Studies in ethnomethodology. Englewood Cliffs NJ, Prentice Hall.

Georgeff, M.P. (1983) Communication and interaction in multi-agent planning. Proc. AAAI-83. Morgan Kaufmann.

Georgeff, M.P. (1984) A theory of action for multi-agent Planning. Proc AAAI-84. Morgan Kaufmann.

Georgeff, M.P. (1986) The Representation of Events in Multi-Agent domains. Proc. AAAI 86. Morgan Kaufmann.

Greif, I. (ed) (1988) Computer supported cooperative work: a book of readings. Morgan Kaufmann.

Hayward S.A., Wielinga B., Breuker J.A. (1987) Structured analysis of knowledge. International Journal of Man-Machine studies 26, 487-498.

Hewitt, C.E. (1986) Offices are open systems. ACM Transcations on Office Information Systems 4(3).

Janis, I.L. (1982) Groupthink: psychological studies of policy decisions and fiascoes. Boston, Houghton Mifflin.

Johnson-Lenz, P., Johnson-Lenz, T., & Hessman, J.F. (1980) JEDEC/EIES computer conferencing for standardization activities. In Henderson, M. (ed) Electronic communication: technology and impacts. AAAS selected symposium 52, Westview Press, Boulder.

Kalin, T., Lubich, H. & Rugelj, J. (1990) A proposal for the architectural model for CSCW systems. WG3 Working Document. Co-Tech Project (COST 14).

Kaye A.R. & Karam G.M. (1987) Cooperating knowledge-based assistants for the office. ACM Transactions on Office Information Systems 5, 297-326.

Kedziersky B. (1982) Communication and management support in system development environments. Proceedings of the conference on human factors in computer systems, Gaithersburg MD, ACM Press.

Kornfeld, W.A. & Hewitt, C.E. (1981) The scientific community metaphor. IEEE Transactions on Systems Man and Cybernetics, SMC (1)1.

Kuna, M. & Klehn, N. (1991) A three-level approach to model systems for CSCW. In Gorling, K. & Sattler (eds) International workshop on CSCW. Institut fur Informatik und Rechentechnik, Berlin.

Laird J.E., Rosenbloom P., Newell A. (1987) SOAR: an architecture for general intelligence. Artificial Intelligence 33.

Langley P., Thompson K., Iba W., Gennari J., Allen J. (1990) An integrated cognitive architecture for autonomous agents. In Van de Velde, W. (ed) "Toward Learning Robots", MIT Press, Cambridge MA.

Lee, J. (1990) SIBYL: a tool for managing group design rationale. In Bikson, T.K. Proceedings of the conference on computer supported cooperative work, Los Angeles. ACM Press, New York.

Lesser, V.R. & Corkill, D. (1981) Functionally accurate cooperative distributed systems. IEEE Transactions on Systems, Man and Cybernetics SMC-11 (1).

Levin, J.A. & Moore, J.A. (1977) Dialogue games: metacommunication structures for natural language interaction. Cognitive Science 1, 395-420.

Levinson, S.C. (1983) Pragmatics. Cambridge University Press.

Lewis, D.K. (1969) Convention: a philosophical study. Harvard University Press.

Malone, T.W., Grant, K.R., Lai, K-Y., Rao, R. & Rosenblitt, D. (1987) Semi-structured messages are surprisingly useful for computer-supported coordination. ACM TOOIS 5(2), 115-131.

McKendree, J.D. (1977) Decision process in crisis management: computers in a new role. In Belzer, J. (ed) Encyclopedia of computer science and technology, Vol 7. Marcel-Dekker.

Minton S., Knoblock C.A., Kuokka D.R., Gil Y., Carbonell J.G. (1988) Prodigy 1.0. The Manual and Tutorial. Report de la Universidad Carnegie Mellon Computer Science Department.

MultiG (1991) A collaborative research program on distributed multimedia applications and gigabit networks. Sundblad, Y. (ed) Proceedings of the 3rd MultiG workshop. KTH Press, Stockholm.

Newell A. (1982) The Knowledge Level. Artificial Intelligence 18, 87-127.

Newell A., Simon H. (1963) GPS: A Program that Simulates Human Thought. In Feigenbaum & Feldman (eds) "Computers and Thought" McGraw Hill.

Newell, A. & Simon, H.A. (1972) Human Problem Solving. Prentice Hall.

Nilsson, N.J. (1980) Principles of artificial intelligence. Palo Alto CA, Tioga; Springer Verlag 1982.

ODP Reference Model. (1990) Basic reference model of open distributed processing (ODP). Requirements for structures and functions. Working document ISO/IECJTC1/SC21/WG7 N308, October 1990.

Opper, S. (1988) A groupware toolbox. BYTE December 275-282.

Power, R.J.D. (1974) A computer model of conversation. Ph.D. thesis, University of Edinburgh.

Power, R.J.D. (1979) The organization of purposeful dialogues. Linguistics 17, 107-152.

Pruitt, D.G. (1981) Negotiation behaviour. New York, Academic Press.

Reder, S. & Schwab, R.G. (1990) The temporal structure of cooperative activity. In Bikson, T.K. Proceedings of the conference on computer supported cooperative work, Los Angeles. ACM Press, New York.

Rice, A.K. (1958) Productivity and social organization: the Ahmedabad experiment. London, Tavistock.

Rosenschein, J.S. & Genesereth, M.R. (1987) Communication and cooperation among logic-based agents. Proceedings of the Sixth Phoenix Conference on Computers and Communications, 594-600.

Sacks, H., Schegloff, E. & Jefferson G. (1974) A simplest systematics for the organization of turn taking in conversation. Language 50(4), 696-735.

Sathi, A., Morton, T.E., & Roth, S.F. (1986) Callisto: an intelligent project management system. AI magazine, Winter 34-52.

Schegloff, E. (1968) Sequencing in conversational openings. American anthropologist 70(4), 1075-1095.

Schegloff, E. & Sacks, H. (1973) Opening up closings. Semiotica 8(4), 289-327.

Searle, J.R. (1969) Speech acts. Cambridge University Press.

Searle, J.R. (1975) A taxonomy of illocutionary acts. In Gunderson, K. (ed) Language, mind and knowledge, 344-369. Minneapolis: University of Minnesota Press.

Shepherd, A., Mayer, N. & Kuchinsky, A. (1990) Strudel: an extensible electronic conversation toolkit. In Bikson, T.K. Proceedings of the conference on computer supported cooperative work, Los Angeles.

Smith R.G. & Davis, R. (1981) Frameworks for cooperation in distributed problem solving. IEEE Transactions on Systems, Man and Cybernetics SMC-11(1), 61-70.

Sproull, L. & Kiesler, S. (1986) Reducing social context cues: electronic mail in organizational communication. Management science 32(11) 1492-1512.

Stefik, M., Foster, G., Bobrow, D., Kahn, K., Lanning, S., & Suchman, L. (1987) Beyond the chalkboard: computer support for collaboration and problem solving in meetings. CACM 30(1), 32-47.

Stoner, J. (1961) A comparison of individual and group decisions involving risk. Master's thesis, MIT Sloan school of industrial management.

Thomas, R.H., Forsdick, H.C., Crowley, T.R., Schaaf R.W., Tomlinson, R.S., Travers, V.M., & Robertson G.G. (1985) Diamond: a multimedia message system built on a distributed architecture. IEEE Computer 18(12) 65-78.

Toulmin, S. (1969) The uses of argument. Cambridge University Press.

Turoff, M. (1972) Delphi conferencing: computer based conferencing with anonymity. J. Tech. Forecasting and Social Change 27(4) 257-373.

Watabe, K., Sakata, S., Maeno, K., Fukuoka, H. & Ohmori, T. (1990) Distributed multi-party desktop conferencing: MERMAID. In Bikson, T.K. Proceedings of the conference on computer supported cooperative work, Los Angeles. ACM Press, New York.

Winograd, T. & Flores, F. (1986) Understanding computers and cognition: a new foundation for design. Norwood, New Jersey: Ablex.

Winograd, T. (1988) A language/action perspective on the design of cooperative work. Human Computer Interaction 3, 3-30.

Zinn, K.L., Parnes, R. & Hench, H. (1976) Computer-based educational communication at the University of Michigan. Proceedings 31st ACM national conference.

Authors' addresses

Paolo Amadio, EMMEPI srl - Fiatimpresit, Viale Italia 1, I-20099 Sesto San Giovanni, Milano, Italy.

Lorella Carminati, Artificial Intelligence Software spa, Via Rombon 11, I-20134 Milano, Italy.

Professor José Cuena, Universidad Politécnica de Madrid, Department of Artificial Intelligence, Campus Montegancedo s/n, Boadilla del Monte, E-28660 Madrid, Spain.

Boudewijn D'Hauwers, Babbage Institute for Knowledge and Information Technology (BIKIT), Plateaustraat 22, B-9000 Ghent, Belgium.

Ilario Fassina, Lombardia Informatica spa, Via Frigia 27, I-20126 Milano, Italy.

Ana García-Serrano, Universidad Politécnica de Madrid, Department of Artificial Intelligence, Campus Montegancedo s/n, Boadilla del Monte, E-28660 Madrid, Spain.

Jonny Jager, ERICSSON Telecomunicaciones S.A., R&D Centre, Telémaco 5, E-28027 Madrid, Spain.

Mike Martin, Mari Group, Mari House, Old Town Hall, Gateshead, Tyne and Wear NE8 1HE, Great Britain.

Graeme Oswald, Mari Group, Mari House, Old Town Hall, Gateshead, Tyne and Wear NE8 1HE, Great Britain.

Encarnaciòn Pastor, ETSI Telecomunicaciòn, Ciudad Universitaria, E-28040 Madrid, Spain.

Richard Power, Artificial Intelligence Software spa, Via Rombon 11, I-20134 Milano, Italy.

Fernand VanDamme, Babbage Institute for Knowledge and Information Technology (BIKIT), Plateaustraat 22, B-9000 Ghent, Belgium.

Veerle Van Hyfte, Babbage Institute for Knowledge and Information Technology (BIKIT), Plateaustraat 22, B-9000 Ghent, Belgium.